Fourth Edition

The ADULT STUDENT'S Guide to
Survival & Success

also by Al Siebert:

The Survivor Personality: Why Some People Are Stronger, Smarter, and More Skillful at Handling Life's Difficulties . . . and How You Can Be, Too

Student Success: How to Succeed in College and Still Have Time for Your Friends (co-authors: Timothy L. Walter and Laurence Smith)

also by Al Siebert and Mary Karr:

Teaching College Success, Career Success, & Internet Skills to Adult Learners (contributing editor: Bernadine Gilpin). An instructor's manual to accompany *The Adult Student's Guide to Survival and Success,* (4th ed.)

Fourth Edition

The ADULT STUDENT'S *Guide to*
Survival & Success

Contributing editor: Barbara Ritter, M.Ed.

Practical Psychology Press, Portland, Oregon

Practical Psychology Press
P.O. Box 535
Portland, Oregon 97207
http://www.thrivenet.com/press/

Book design/prepress by Kristin Pintarich
Cover design by Heidi Barnes
Printed with soy ink by Thomson-Shore, Inc.

10 9 8 7 6 5 4 3 2

Publisher's Cataloging in Publication
(Prepared by Quality Books Inc.)

Siebert, Al, 1934- .
    The adult student's guide to survival & success
/ Al Siebert & Bernadine Gilpin & Mary B. Karr ;
contributing editor, Barbara Ritter. -- 4th ed.
        p.   cm.
    Includes bibliographical references and index.
    LCCN: 99-75218
    ISBN: 0-944227-20-1

    1. College student orientation--United States.
2. Study skills. 3. Adult learning--United
States.   I. Gilpin, Bernadine. II. Karr, Mary B.,
1938- III. Ritter, Barbara. IV. Title.

LB2343.32.S54 2000   378.1'9

Contents

1   *Lots of Help Is Available* *1*

2   *Fears and Concerns: How to Confront*
     and Overcome Them *9*

3   *How to Choose Your Program,*
     Get Financial Help, and Become Oriented *20*

4   *How to Succeed in College* *34*

5   *The Best Way to Study* *43*

6   *How to Get High Grades on Tests* *61*

7   *How to Write Excellent Papers* *75*

8   *Learning Styles and Teaching Styles:*
     How to Influence Instructors *87*

9   *Your Family and Friends:*
     How to Gain Their Support and Encouragement *100*

10   *How to Balance Going*
     to College with Working *110*

11   *Celebrating Diversity* *118*

12   *How to Handle Pressure Well* *126*

13   *Resiliency in a World of Non-Stop Change* *135*

     Resources and Selected Reading *149*

     Online Resources *154*

     Index *162*

     About the Authors *166*

     Feedback Request *167*

*To all students
with the courage and commitment
to pursue their dreams*

Foreword

If you haven't been in school for a while, you probably feel nervous and have doubts about your ability to succeed in college. Guess what. We felt the same way when we first started!

Al attended college as a veteran on the GI Bill of Rights. Bernadine started college at age 35 with five young children. Mary started college when the youngest of her four children entered high school. Our personal experiences helped shape what we put into the book.

The first version of this book was published in 1982. Since then, thousands of adult students have found it extremely helpful. Many say they couldn't have made it through college without *The Adult Student's Guide*.

This revised fourth edition has the kind of practical information that comes from experience. It will help you deal with all your concerns and more. It shows how to study effectively, pass tests, write good papers, and get high grades. It is loaded with suggestions for handing all the challenges that can block your progress. And with this edition we emphasize how the skills you need for succeeding in college are the same skills most employers want today.

Mainly, we would say that if you believe in yourself and take things one day at a time, you can get the education you want. You have faced up to tough challenges before. You can survive the late nights studying, taking tests, and writing papers. With good effort you can succeed in college. If we did it, we believe you can too!

Al Siebert
Bernadine Gilpin
Mary B. Karr

Chapter 1

Lots of Help Is Available

Do you know that at most colleges the average age of students is over 30 and over half the students work while going to school?

Do you know that your college provides many free services to help you succeed?

Do you know that the abilities you use to succeed in college are the same abilities that employers look for?

Have you heard that many employers now value emotional intelligence (EQ) higher than IQ?

Your Path to Your Future

If you are like most adult students, you feel both excited and anxious about starting college. The exciting part is that college is the pathway to new skills, a new career, and a better future. College is much more than a place to learn new information or get a degree, however. It is where you learn how to learn and how to continue learning all your life.

Going to college is like venturing into a new world. It is a journey to a different life. But, like any adventure that carries risks, it can stir up anxiety and fears.

Some Normal Fears, Concerns, and Feelings

Do you feel nervous about going to college? Concerned that your brain is rusty and that you won't be able to keep up with younger students? Feel overwhelmed by all the emphasis on computer skills, the internet, and rapidly changing technology? Afraid that you can't afford college, and don't see how you can work and go to college and raise your family? Feel guilty about depriving others while you do something that feels selfish?

If so, welcome to the club! You are normal. As you get to know your fellow students, you will learn that most adult college students feel these same fears and concerns.

If you have enrolled in college because getting an education is something you've dreamed about, your path will be easier. Working to fulfill your dreams can help motivate you to keep going through difficult times. You still will have challenges, however.

Adult students facing the biggest challenges are usually those who feel forced by circumstances to take college classes. It's tough to feel motivated to study when you feel angry about being "downsized" or have been forced by divorce back into the workforce. Losing your job through no fault of your own or being divorced and impoverished with few job skills carries additional emotional challenges to cope with—but they can be handled! We'll show how.

No matter what your motives for taking classes, the guidelines and suggestions in this book will give you a very good chance of succeeding in getting the education you want and need.

How *The Adult Student's Guide* Will Help You Reach Your Career Goals

Every chapter in this book contains valuable information about how to succeed in college after you have been away from school for a while. It will show you how to succeed even if you have a family, work, have many responsibilities, and need time to spend with friends .

Most adult students take college courses to improve their career opportunities. *The Adult Student's Guide* contains many useful suggestions on how to be highly desirable to employers. (*Translation: hired quickly and paid well.*) Getting a diploma or a degree is not enough, however, in today's world. Employers in today's world of non-stop change are looking for people with college degrees who can prove that they:

+ can work well in teams
+ are self-motivated to learn new skills
+ have good communications skills
+ don't have negative attitudes
+ have good computer skills
+ are not "technophobic"
+ can work without a detailed job description
+ do not need constant supervision
+ provide excellent customer service
+ use common sense to solve problems
+ hold up well under pressure
+ are resilient and handle change well
+ do consistently high-quality work

To help you develop abilities that will give you an advantage in the competition for better jobs and help you reach higher levels of success on the job, we have included many suggestions on how to develop and *document* the abilities listed above. You will find, for example, guidelines on how to work in "learning teams," tips on how to improve communications skills, coaching on how to be highly resilient, and guidelines on how to develop a portfolio of accomplishments.

The Adult Student Online

Computer literacy used to be the new skill that employers required. Now, if you are going to be competitive in this technology age, internet skills are essential. We revised this fourth edition of *The Adult Student's Guide* to give you many opportunities to go online to practice and develop your internet skills.

The Adult Student's Guide is the first "student success" book designed to be interactive with its own web site. Almost every chapter has additional information and updated resources at our Adult Student web site. You can access this site at **http://www.adultstudent.com/**. Throughout the book whenever you see the symbol ⏛ you will find a file or resource at the web site.

Chapter Contents

The first half of the book covers academic challenges. It shows how you, as an adult student, can handle the challenges successfully. *The second half* covers non-academic challenges that can prevent you from succeeding in college and in your career if you do not handle them well.

Chapter 2 shows how to confront and overcome many fears and concerns expressed by adult students. It answers most of the questions that adult students ask. (If your question isn't answered in the book, ask us at the adult student web site!)

Chapter 3 shows how to make certain you are in the right educational program, get financing, and get oriented. Did you know that financial aid is available for adult students? Even part-time students? Chapter three (and the web site) has information on how to finance your education.

Chapter 4 explains how to succeed in your courses. It shows how to find out what is required in each course, how to organize your notebooks, and how to take lecture notes.

Chapter 5 shows how to manage your time and how to study using a very effective study method. Here you will learn how to reach a study goal, stop studying, and reward yourself. Self-motivated people must learn how to be self-stoppers!

Nervous about taking tests? **Chapter 6** shows how to prepare for all kinds of tests, so that you feel confident, less nervous, and score higher than you suspected you could.

Term papers are always a challenge. In **Chapter 7** you will find efficient and effective ways to research and write papers that get top grades.

Chapter 8 shows how your learning style may create conflicts between you and your instructors. It shows what to do about these mismatches and how to influence all kinds of instructors.

In **Chapter 9** you will find many practical tips on how to gain cooperation, support, and encouragement from your family, friends, and employers.

Most adult students work. **Chapter 10** shows how to combine working with taking college courses. Many employers offer special work schedules and reimbursement for courses completed. If you need to find a job to support yourself, or searching for a new career, we have many good suggestions at the adult student web site.

Your ability to understand and work with people from diverse cultures and backgrounds can help or hinder your career. **Chapter 11** shows how cultural diversity in your classes can lead to better relationships and work team competencies in the workplace.

Feeling pressured to get more work done in less time? **Chapter 12** explains effective ways to handle pressure, reduce stress, and develop inner strengths.

Could you succeed in a job that does not have a job description? **Chapter 13** shows how to be resilient in this world of nonstop change, gain strength from adversity, and develop professionalism in what you do.

At the end of most chapters you will find:
+ An **Action Review** checklist for reviewing how well you are putting into action what the chapter covered.
+ **Support Group Activities** that will enhance your learning.
+ Suggestions for an **Accomplishments Portfolio**.

Create a Support Group and Team Up with "Study Buddies"

Research into understanding why some people handle stress and difficult challenges better than others shows that the people who cope best have good support groups. Your college may provide a seminar for new students. If you can arrange to take one of these seminars your chances of succeeding in college will increase.

If you can't fit a college success seminar into your schedule, we still want to encourage you to create your own support group or find a "study buddy." You'll be less lonely, develop good friendships, help each other through tough moments, and increase your chances of succeeding in college. You will find guidelines for creating a support group in Chapter 2.

Your Accomplishments Portfolio

You probably know that artists, models, and photographers have portfolios to show their work. Nowadays, because employers are overwhelmed by job applications, the applicants with the best chance of getting interviewed submit a one page summary outlining what they have documented in their portfolio of accomplishments.

Employment interviewers need your help! They appreciate and are impressed when someone has empathy for them. A one page summary of what is in your portfolio gets their attention.

Today's employers are looking for abilities not usually covered by traditional application forms and resumes. At the end of most chapters, you will find suggestions for creating a file of evidence that documents your ability to:

+ be a team member in a culturally diverse group,
+ communicate well,
+ problem-solve difficult challenges,
+ research ideas,
+ use computers and software programs,

- ✦ do consistently excellent work,
- ✦ function well in constant change,
- ✦ hold up under pressure keeping a good attitude,
- ✦ reach your goals, and
- ✦ are self-motivated to continuously develop new skills.

Student portfolios are becoming so common that many colleges now provide their students with a portfolios web site. With this arrangement, employers can go online to examine various accomplishments you have documented at your college web site.

To provide you with valuable guidelines we have enlisted the help of Barbara Ritter, one of the pioneers in developing student portfolios. The steps she describes for creating an excellent portfolio would take too much space here, so we have placed her guidelines on how to create an accomplishments portfolio at our web site.

⌇ Look for the file "Your Accomplishments Portfolio" at
http://www.adultstudent.com/

You are Special as a Student

Have you noticed that when you tell people about going to college they treat you differently? When Mary Karr started college she noticed an immediate change in how people treated her. She says:

> Before I started college, when my husband and I went to a party or social gathering, people would ask what I did. When I told them I was a housewife raising four children they'd say, "Oh," and start talking to someone else. On a scale from 1 to 100, I felt like I rated about a 3. After I enrolled, when people found out I was a college student, they'd say, "Oh!" I got treated like I had something important to say. My rating soared to the high nineties. The difference was fantastic!

Another student reported that he needed to change his working hours by half an hour to make a night class. He hesitated about approaching his supervisor, but finally spoke up. He asked for what he needed and explained why. From that day on his supervisor took a more personal interest in him and asked frequently about how school was going. Being a student can have some unexpected dividends!

The World Wants You to Succeed

Going to college is an exciting challenge. It will take hard work and some sacrifices but the benefits are worth the effort. The main point to understand is that you are not alone. There are many people and many resources available to you. The world wants you to succeed in your effort to better yourself!

Chapter 2

Fears and Concerns: How to Confront and Overcome Them

Have you wondered if some of your fears about going to college are unrealistic?

Do you know that instructors enjoy teaching adult students and adult students often get high grades?

Do you know that colleges, universities, and company training programs go out of their way to help adult students enroll and succeed?

Do you know you increase your chances of succeeding in college when you participate in a support group?

So, I finally dragged myself over to the community college and took two courses. And, I was scared to death. I had been at war, in police riots, and a firefighter and that was all right. But, now I'm going to this college and I'm scared to death. I literally had stomach cramps—got physically sick. I really don't know why I was scared. I had no idea...no reason...it had nothing to do with anything...there was no consequence to pay...I could have gone over there, flunked out, and nothing would have happened. I would still have been a lieutenant in the fire department. Nothing would have changed. As it turned out, I left there with a 4.0 after taking four courses. But, when I first went through the door, I was dying.   —*Bob DePrato*

Facing Your Fears Takes Courage

In this book we will show you how thousands of people just like you found the courage to overcome their fears and succeed in college. We will show you how to develop the skills you need to increase your confidence. We will show you how to locate and use resources you never knew existed.

You may doubt your ability to succeed in college if you have not studied or taken tests for a long time, if you have to work, or have other responsibilities. It is possible, however, to be a successful college student and still handle other commitments.

You have overcome fears in the past by facing up to them and seeking information. You can do the same now. Before reading farther, take a minute to indicate how strong or weak your fear is about the following.

Strong—5 Moderately strong—4 Medium—3 Mild—2 Weak—1

1. __ I can't compete with younger students.
2. __ I won't be able to learn, my brain is rusty.
3. __ I can't do well in math.
4. __ I won't be able to study well.
5. __ I don't know how to use computers.
6. __ Instructors dislike older students.

7. __ I won't fit in.
8. __ I won't have time for my family and other interests.
9. __ I can't afford college.
10. __ I can't work and study and raise a family.
11. __ My family will feel neglected.
12. __ Going part time will take me too long.

Common Fears and Concerns of Adult Students

If your total score from the above list is over 30 you definitely need to look through the following list of fears and concerns. They are typically felt and experienced by most adult students starting college. And like many fears you have experienced in your life, many of these fears are not realistic either.

I haven't studied in years. I'm out of practice. My brain feels rusty.
    There is no evidence that older students can't learn and remember as well as younger students. This book will show you how to take notes, remember information from lectures and texts, and pass tests as well as any younger student.

I'm not sure I can read, write, or do math well enough to take college courses.
    The college is happy to give you a free assessment of your skill levels to advise you what courses are best suited for you. If you need brush-up courses, they are available.

    Even dyslexic and other "learning disabled" students can succeed in college.

-√- For more information see the section on Learning
    Disabilities at our web site:
    http://www.adultstudent.com/

I was always nervous taking tests in high school. I'll be too upset to do well.
    There is plenty of help available to show you how to reduce your anxieties about taking tests. College counseling and study skills centers provide help for students who need to learn techniques of test taking. Ask around.

I was so nervous the first day of classes that I arrived at school 45 minutes ahead of the 9:00 class time. It was OK though, because I needed the time to keep running into the rest room—bladders seem so insistent sometimes. As I walked into the room for my first class I realized that my legs were shaking so hard I could barely walk. Fortunately, the front seat nearest the door was available so I quickly sat down. I tried to remain calm, but I knew I was trembling—my hands just wouldn't stop. After a *very* long time, the teacher came in and was ready to start the class. The first thing I noticed was how young she was and I thought to myself that school was going to be harder than I had imagined because how could this very young woman (she looked like a student herself) ever understand someone my age. Then I noticed that her legs were shaking! *She was nervous! Wonderful!* My day changed and was grand from then on. Oh yes,—I also found out that she was a graduate teaching assistant and that she was very sympathetic to all students. —MK

I won't be able to compete. Only a few smart students receive high grades.

Times have changed! In the past many instructors graded "on the curve." They gave high marks to the few students who scored better than others in the class. Now, however, most instructors grade students on how much learning they accomplish during a course. Further, in many courses you will work on team projects with other students. This means that you and other students work together to master the material and all get excellent grades.

Don't be embarrassed if you can't do everything quickly.
Don't try to compete with the young—compete with yourself.
—Eva Corazon Fernando-Lumba, age 78
(Chosen by her college classmates to be the class speaker at commencement.)

I feel like a misfit, like an outsider in a strange world. I won't fit in.
The faculty, administrators, and students will be more friendly and helpful than you might imagine. Many younger students enjoy having older friends from whom they can learn and exchange views and experiences. Making friends like this can be some of the most enriching of your educational experiences. Besides, remind yourself that your tax dollars may have helped build the place. You have a right to be there.

Instructors won't like having an older student in class.
Instructors enjoy adult students. They welcome the life experience older students offer to a class. They expect to find communication is easier with you. Returning students are frequently more motivated to learn and pay closer attention to the instructor. Studies show older students tend to get better grades than younger students.

I can't afford college.
Most students qualify for some sort of financial aid. This may be in the form of scholarships, loans, grants, or employer reimbursements. And did you know that programs now exist where you can earn college credit for working? We will cover this in more detail in Chapter 3. College administrators and counselors are aware of the financial dilemmas facing returning students and will assist you in obtaining financial help. (See Resources and Suggested Readings.)

I'm retired, I'd like to attend a few classes but I can't afford the tuition.
Many colleges allow older citizens to take classes at reduced fees, if space is available. You won't get credit for the course, but you can *audit* or attend classes at minimal cost. Look in the Sources section at the back of this book for where to write for information about 1500 colleges and universities that offer free or reduced tuition to older students.

I have young children, but I can't afford the cost of child care. How can I attend classes with children to raise?

Colleges are accommodating the needs of returning students. There are child care referral services at many colleges and women's resource centers. Many campuses offer low-cost child-care services for students. Colleges are doing much to assist people who have children. With young children it is very important to select healthful, reliable child care arrangements. Many student parents trade baby-sitting with other students, friends, family, or neighbors. Most colleges offer classes at night and on weekends. To work out a cooperative schedule one student takes day classes, the other night time or weekend classes. Some student parents vary days of the week with one taking classes on Monday, Wednesday, Friday, the other on Tuesdays and Thursdays. You can also inquire about courses available on video tapes at a learning center. You go through the material at your own speed at a time that is convenient to you.

I don't think I can physically attend classes at the college campus.

There are some courses offered by modem on your computer or by the electronic classroom via satellite. Do you know that some college courses can be taken at home by watching broadcasts on television? Do you know that the college of your choice probably has correspondence or home study courses available? Inquire. You may be in for a pleasant surprise.

I cannot attend full time. It is hard to imagine all the years it will take to get a college degree.

A long journey starts with the first step. Once you become adjusted to being a student and gain confidence, you will probably be able to take more courses each term. In some cases, your life experiences and skills can be counted as credit toward your degree. In the next chapter you will see there are three ways to obtain college credit for what you already know, without taking courses. Or you might consider a shorter program. Many colleges offer two-year programs for people training for specific careers such as an associate degree in nursing. Regardless of the program you take, most students say their college careers go much faster than they thought possible.

My friends and family will suffer if I have to spend lots of time with schoolwork and my partner may feel threatened by my attempt to improve myself?

You will probably be surprised at how much your family and friends will support you in your new role as a student. Explain to them why you need to return to school. Show how your success will benefit all of you. Give them a chance and they will probably be very encouraging. Chapter 9 has a number of practical suggestions.

I have a heavy load at work. I have too many pressures to take college courses.

Did you know that many college courses are offered one evening a week? If you are willing to give up one evening a week you can take a college course. Employers are often willing to adjust workloads for employees in college, see Chapter 10. The time management tips in Chapter 5 will help. For guidelines on dealing with stress and pressure, read Chapter 12. The solution is to decide what you want in life and go for it.

If I become a student, I'll never have time for my family, friends, or outside interests. I can't take courses, study, and still have time for anything else.

It is true that you won't be able to do everything you did before and also be a college student. You will have to make some changes. But millions of people have gone to college while working and maintaining active personal lives. You are no different. If you follow the guidelines for succeeding in college, you'll do just fine and still have time for other important things.

I won't know anyone and I'm afraid to start out on my own.

Finding a "study buddy" will help you overcome those

feelings quickly. It will not be long before you have supportive friends in each class, friendly fellow students who will help you feel you really belong and can succeed.

Anything is Possible...

As you can see, there are ways to handle most of your concerns about being a college student. Many fears disappear when you confront them. As other fears or concerns develop, here are the steps to follow:

+ First identify exactly what your fear or concern is. Write it down or describe it to someone. Then ask, "Is my worry based on rumors, or opinions, or is it a result of known facts?"
+ To cope with problems or difficulties that might occur, ask other adult college students about their experiences. Find out if your fears are real.
+ With specific, realistic problems, talk to an academic advisor or a college counselor. They will help you develop a realistic plan of action coping with the problem. Remember: *Don't be afraid to ask questions!*

Let Us Know!

—⋀— Do you have other concerns? Suggestions for other students? Please let us know at our Adult Student web site: http://www.adultstudent.com/

Colleges and Company Training Programs Want You!

In the last few years higher education has changed. Colleges are spending a lot of money to attract and retain older students. Colleges arrange financial aid, employment, transportation (car pools and buses), housing, child care, personal counseling, medical coverage, and classes on how to study efficiently and pass courses. They provide counselors and advisors, recreational activities, and much more.

Did you know that many companies are scrambling to find employees with employable skills? These companies will often pay trainees to take college courses, provide fringe benefits, and guarantee better jobs to graduates.

Now is a wonderful time to obtain a college education. Students of any age who want an education, advanced skills, or new careers can find support, resources, and encouragement.

How to Create a Support Group and Team Up With a "Study Buddy"

+ Get together with a few other beginning students. Urge several new students that seem "lost" to come along, but don't have more than six or seven in the group.

+ Meet in a place where you can sit comfortably and talk with each other. The college cafeteria is a good place and has snacks and beverages available.

+ Introduce yourselves. Take turns talking about your feelings, impressions, and experiences starting college. Keep making sure you have each other's names right as you talk and listen.

+ Find out why you each decided to go to college. Talk about your dreams and plans for the future. Ask about difficulties that you have to handle.

+ Ask about the courses you are each taking. Find out what program each person has selected or is considering.

+ Make certain each person feels heard. By the time you finish, make certain each of you feels "A few of my classmates know about me and understand what I am feeling and experiencing right now."

+ Discuss the benefits from having a small support group. Talk about why it could be useful to get together to problem solve difficulties, encourage each other, and applaud your successes.

+ If several of you think you would benefit from studying together and reading each other's papers, form a special "study buddy" group. Adult students usually have many activities that keep them isolated, but a study buddy can be a great way to keep each other going.

✦ Plan to meet again soon to discuss what you are learning in this book about how to succeed in college. Read ahead, for example, on how to gain support from family and discuss what you are each doing.

✦ Congratulate each other for having the courage to take this exciting, important step in life.

Support Group Hints for Success

Why should we form a support group rather than just getting together with a couple of people whenever we can?

Well, you've heard about the road that is paved with good intentions. Getting together is fine for providing a relaxed social meeting, but after the first couple of weeks busy people just don't have time to chat for more than a few minutes. By committing yourself and others to a set time and place and agenda for what you are going to discuss, everyone will be more likely to continue to participate. The outcome of your support group meetings should provide each member with results that will help each of you be successful in your college classes.

Does our support group need a group leader?

Probably not in a formal sense, but groups fall apart quickly when no one is responsible for some of the tasks. One way to run a support group is to have everyone be the leader for a week or a month. That person should have specific responsibilities for his/her time of leadership. Some leader responsibilities are:

✦ Inform everyone of the meeting day and time
✦ Start meetings on time
✦ Introduce discussion topics
✦ Keep discussions on track
✦ Set day and time for next meeting
✦ Set agenda for next meeting

What about a recorder?

It's nice to have a group record about what was discussed. Also, if someone misses one meeting, the group record will provide him/her with the notes. As with the group leader job, the job of recorder could rotate each week or month.

How often should we meet?

The support group will need to decide when, where, and how often to meet. Once a week works best for most adult students. Meeting more often can get complicated as the demands of classes start to increase. Every two weeks might work, but meeting less frequently than that will lose the continuity that regular meetings provide.

Is there anything else we should do?

You should know how to contact everyone. Exchange phone numbers, fax numbers, postal and e-mail addresses. Find out the best way to contact each person.

Support Group Activities

1. Talk with each other about your fears and concerns. Then discuss how you can overcome or eliminate the fears and barriers. Keep in mind that some problems can't be eliminated, but it helps to talk with people who understand.
2. Discuss the difference between academic and non-academic challenges that concern you. Write your own list, then develop a plan for dealing with each item on your list.
3. Ask each other about difficult challenges that you've each dealt with in the past. Ask for examples of being resilient and how you were made stronger and more self-confident by rough experiences. These memories will help remind you that you have the inner strength to not only cope well, but be made stronger and better by adversity.
4. Tell each other about your work experiences with managers or co-workers who were bright, but lacked emotional intelligence about people. Discuss what it means to be emotionally intelligent and why it is so important.

Chapter 3

How to Choose Your Program, Get Financial Help, and Become Oriented

Have you heard that you can turn some of your life experiences into college credit?

Do you know where to inquire about financial aid?

Do you know you can probably get financial aid if you need it?

Do you know where to go with questions about class schedules, transportation, health services or security?

Getting Enrolled and Registered

What Courses Do You Want to Take?
The first thing to do is get a copy of the college catalog. Take your time looking through it.

You'll need to know what's ahead of you and what courses you will have to take. The college catalog describes all the courses offered and explains which ones you will be required to take if you want to receive a degree or certificate. Read the fine print carefully.

> ⚫➤ NOTE: *The college catalog is a kind of contract.* The college agrees to award you a degree if you do all the required work as indicated in the catalog you used for your initial enrollment into degree coursework. Keep a copy for future reference.

If a course sounds interesting, but is in a program for people majoring in that area, you might have to take a prerequisite course before taking the one you desire. A *prerequisite* course is one that students must take and complete before they can get into a more advanced course.

Some courses are so popular, there are many classes during the day with many instructors. If you have a choice, find out which instructors other students recommend and why they recommend them. Keep in mind, however, that an easy teacher may not be the best for your future You are here to get a solid education, not just a degree.

Once you know the courses you want, look at the schedule of classes. The *schedule* will tell you the time, location, and instructor for each course. If you do not find that a course you want is available at this time, contact the department. Ask the secretary when the course you want will be offered next and who will teach it. Department secretaries are a gold mine of information. Not every course is offered every term or semester, so it might be practical to outline a two year schedule for yourself at this time.

Computer Enhanced, Web-Based (Online), and Distance Learning Courses

Computer Enhanced Courses: Many college instructors are using computers to aid in the teaching of their courses. The instructor may post course outlines, notes, supplemental materials, self-tests and other aids that can assist with student learning at the college web site. You can access these pages from your home computer or from computers on campus. Many local libraries also have computers for your use if you do not have your own.

Web-based or Online Courses: Online courses are taught by instructors and function like a regular classroom. The main difference is that you "go to class" using your computer and your instructor teaches the class using his or her computer. Online classes are asynchronous, meaning that teacher and students "arrive" and "leave" on their own individual time schedule. Usually, assignments, discussions, etc., are to be completed by a specific time each week. One student may visit class and post assignments at 3:15 a.m., while others are in and out all through the day and evening. Online classes require a password that allows only registered student to access the class.

Distance Learning Courses: Distance Learning classes are usually taught once a week. The instructor is at one location that may or may not include some students. Other students are located at one or more locations that are some distance from the instructor. Distance Learning classes, like regular classrooms are "real time," everyone is in class at the same time. The instructor will use audio and video links to hear and see students, and students will watch the instructor on a TV screen. Discussions will include students at all the locations.

Program Choices

Learn how to tell the difference between a credit course, a non-credit course, and a transfer course. A *non-credit* course will not count toward a college degree. A *credit* course leads to a degree or certificate. You cannot earn a college degree by taking non-credit courses. A *transfer* course is a credit course that will be accepted by most four-year colleges if you want your classes to lead to a college degree.

You will need to decide how many courses and how many credit hours you want to try. A full-time student usually takes four or five courses totalling from 12 to 17 credit hours. The college may have a policy limiting the number of hours a student can take.

If you take two or three courses for less than about 12 credit hours, you will be considered a half-time or part-time student, depending on the college.

Community colleges offer *Associate Degree* programs that require about two years taking a full load. These programs include:

+ General Studies—a combination of vocational courses, basic skill building courses, and courses that transfer into four year degree programs at degree granting colleges or universities.
+ Arts/Humanities—transfer courses in writing, journalism, music, speech communication, theater arts.
+ Science—transfer courses in biology, botany, chemistry, geology, math, computer science.
+ Social Science—transfer courses in psychology, sociology, political science, history, geography, economics, women's studies.
+ Vocational certificate programs usually include: nursing, diesel mechanics, dental assistant, computer science, television production, software specialist, internet webmaster, internet associate.

Transfer courses taken at a community college, or enrollment at a four year college or university can lead to the following academic degrees:

Bachelor of Arts (B.A.)—Earned in a four year program emphasizing humanities and arts courses plus a foreign language at an accredited college or university.

Bachelor of Science (B.S.)—Earned in a four year program emphasizing science courses plus advanced level mathematics at an accredited college or university.

Master's degree *(M.A., M.S., M.Ed.)*—Earned after the B.A.

or B.S., taking approximately two years of courses in arts or science and writing a thesis.

Doctorates: Philosophy (Ph.D.), Education (Ed.D.), Psychology (Psy.D.)—Usually earned after the master's degree with advanced, graduate level seminar work and a doctoral thesis based on original research.

Prior Learning Assessment (PLA) Credits

Did you know you can receive college credit for expertise you have acquired? If you ran your own business, for example, and now wish to earn a business degree, PLA credit may be a possibility for you. Some colleges and universities offer prior learning assessment (PLA) credits or other credits for life and work experience.

Educational institutions offering these credits usually have workshops to help you document your learning. A sizeable amount of writing and validation is required but you may be rich in life experience and able to qualify for official college credit.

Ronald, for example, served as a law enforcement officer for many years when he had to leave the force because of an injury. He had taken so many classes and workshops in law enforcement over the years that he received 56 credit hours as a result of a prior learning assessment. His case is unusual but demonstrates what is possible. Most students receive 10 to 20 hours credit for prior learning.

Jane had traveled extensively with her husband, a career military officer. She had visited most of the countries in Europe. She also could speak German fluently. With documented validation she was able to earn college credit in European history, sociology, and foreign language.

Marge wanted to complete a degree in home economics that she had started 25 years previously. She had managed a home, raised three children, and participated in many community service activities. When she read the course descriptions required for her major, she saw that her life experience fit nicely into some of the courses. She contacted an advisor and verified that PLA could be used toward her degree. She attended a class on documenting her experiences and was able to rapidly complete the requirements for a home economics degree.

Credits must be paid for, but when the push of time and experience is on your side it is an option to consider.

College Level Entrance Examination Program (CLEP)

For information about CLEP tests and how to arrange for them ask your college advisor. About 1500 colleges will accept CLEP scores for certain subjects. The subjects may have been studied in an advance course in high school or special training at work. The CLEP score subjects will be recorded on your transcript at your time of admission and count as credit toward graduation. You do not have to pay the college for the credits recorded.

Or You Can Challenge Courses

A third way to get college credit without taking courses is to challenge introductory level courses at the college. A more comprehensive description of the course work can be seen in a Course Content Guide often available through the department secretary. If you believe you already know a subject quite well, and the college allows, you can arrange to take the final examination in a course to see if you can pass it. If you do, you can get credit for the course by paying the normal registration fee. Keep in mind, however, that you may miss out on a valuable foundation for more advanced courses in the subject.

Buy Your Textbooks Early

After you have registered, go to the bookstore and purchase the required textbooks for your courses. In the bookstore each shelf will list the instructor and course that the books are for.

Do not wait until after the first class meeting to buy your books because the bookstore may not have ordered enough books for everyone. They generally expect some students to drop the course and bring books back for a refund.

If you buy a used textbook pay close attention to which edition it is. Purchase only the most recent edition of a textbook. The instructor will not approve of your using a used second edition of a textbook when the third edition is now the one he or she uses.

When you purchase your textbooks keep your receipts and do not put your name in your books, at least not right away. If for any reason the course is cancelled or you do not want to stay in it, you can sell your books back to the bookstore for a full refund within a certain time limit.

Courses Can Be Dropped

If, after attending the first or second class in a course you realize you've made a serious mistake, then consider dropping the class or transferring to another course. Remember, though, *it is normal to feel somewhat overwhelmed by a course at first*. Talk to the instructor or check with an advisor before dropping. If you drop a course early, most of your money may be refunded.

How to Get Financial Help

Financial assistance can be received through federal and state aid programs, scholarships, and loans. This assistance may help you pay the difference between what you can afford to pay and what it will cost you to go to college. Under federal and state aid programs all families and individuals are treated equally by a standardized evaluation of how much you and/or your family can afford to pay. Age is no barrier, but if you are under twenty-four, your parents income will be considered unless you are married or are a single parent.

Scholarships are frequently tailored to specific populations. Many funds are available for minorities and other special populations like displaced homemakers, women over a certain age, or students with special talents or career objectives. Examples include AARP's (American Association of Retired Persons) Women's Initiative 10th Anniversary Scholarship Program for women over fifty, Business & Professional Women's Foundation Scholarship, and the National Women's Relief Corporation. Unions and service clubs like Rotary, Elks, and Kiwanis are also worth investigating.

Loans can be through federal or state funds, private banks, or individuals. Do not forget to talk to family or friends who may feel it is the best investment in the world to help you get an education leading to a brighter future.

These People on Welfare Succeeded

Late one evening, 26 year old Carol sat with her baby in a bus station. Unmarried and on welfare, she had no money to pay for a room. Her life had been very rough. She felt that she was bad, abnormal, awful, and that life had passed her by. At that moment a well dressed woman sat down next to Carol and started talking with her. The woman was a college administrator. She said that she had once been on welfare.

The woman encouraged Carol to seek a college education. Carol had dropped out of school when she ran away from home at age 13. She knew she could not read, write, or do arithmetic very well. Carol went to a college and took some tests. They showed that she was learning disabled. With encouragement, however, she managed to learn basic skills and then pass the high school equivalency test. She obtained public assistance funds to take college courses. She found out how to obtain grants and student loans.

She got off welfare. She took as many courses as the college would allow each term. At age 30 she graduated with a B.A. with honors. Carol went on to earn an M.A. and now helps others find ways to finance their education. (See Sources.)

Gerald was laid off from an International Harvester plant when the farm recession hit in 1982. He applied for work at 380 companies with no success. He became homeless when his unemployment benefits ran out. He moved out of his apartment and lived for months in a rusty 1960 Mercury. When his car "died" he lived on the streets and did odd jobs whenever he could find them.

He heard about the Dislocated Workers Program, applied, and was enrolled in a community college. With financial aid, he became an A level student in accounting at the University of Iowa.

Fill Out the Forms

The office for financial aid has information about many sources of money for college students. Be prepared to fill out lots of forms. The forms can appear so overwhelming to the beginning student that some people walk away and never come back. Don't give up! *Many colleges give workshops in how to fill out the forms.* The financial aid personnel will lead you through the forms step-by-step, if necessary. There also is available at many college campuses a video tape that takes you through the application process.

Many colleges use the financial aid form (FAF) as a way to check eligibility for available scholarships. If you don't qualify this year, be sure to check again. The rules often change. Lack of eligibility one year is not necessarily true the next.

You can get ready to fill out the financial forms by preparing a rough budget of your expenses for the year. Your expenses will include: tuition and fees, books and supplies, room and board, transportation, and personal expenses.

Money is Available in Many Ways

Scholarships are only one form of aid or financial support offered to students. Many programs provide students with grants and loans. The internet can be a big help in accessing data for funds, as well as on-campus financial aid offices. A program called START contains a national database of over 300,000 scholarships, awards, loans, fellowships, and financial aid awards based on merit not financial need. Check the internet for a program called FUND-FINDER which calculates the expected family contribution for college costs and locates approximately 3,000 private and state-sponsored programs. CIS (Career Information Systems) has a scholarship component and it is available in most employment offices. Your willingness to do your "homework" and fill out many application forms can make the difference in finding funds.

Financial Aid Comes in Many Forms

A *grant* is an outright gift. It does not have to be repaid. Financial aid can be in the form of reduced tuition. A growing number of senior citizens are taking advantage of the free or reduced costs for people over 62 or 65 attending state funded colleges.

At some colleges, students without funds may qualify for a reduction in tuition and fees.

Many students qualify for loans at very low interest rates. Most student loans do not have to start to be repaid until after graduation. These funds are available from banks, from the federal government, and other sources.

If you are a veteran, you probably know about your GI benefits provided by the federal government, but do you also know that educational benefits may be provided by your state? The office of financial aid at the college can tell you if you qualify.

The U.S. Department of Education makes funds available to college students through a number of programs. You can apply for funding through the college, at a lending institution, or directly to the Department of Education:

Pell Grants at a community college can go up to $3,000 for the first year for an undergraduate enrolled full-time; there can also be reduced funds available for students who can only enroll part-time. No payback is needed when your courses are successfully completed.

Supplemental Educational Opportunity Grants vary a great deal with the institution. One community college may provide $900 based on your need while a private college may have more funds available. No repayment is required on completion of course work.

Stafford/Ford Loans vary according to need and institution. For independent students a college may loan up to $6,625 the first year, $7,500 the second year, and more in subsequent years up to a total of $46,000. Other colleges with different tuition may increase or decrease this amount.

There are subsidized and non-subsidized loans. *These loans must be paid back* if you stop attending college at least half-time for six months. A payment schedule is available, however. The entire loan does not come due at once.

Perkins Loans vary according to need and institution. Colleges can run out of funds so GET YOUR APPLICATION IN EARLY. Funds awarded can change from year to year.

Other federal programs include federal work study, the

TRIO program, and a multitude of scholarships and grants available for specific fields of study. Each institution is different, so contact your college's financial aid office for the specific funding opportunities they offer.

New Financial Aid Forms (FAF) come out in January for the following academic year. These may be mailed to you on request, or found online, but often a personal appointment with a financial aid officer can give you current and exact information for your institution. Sometimes it can pay to shop different colleges and see where you can get the best financial aid package.

Don't Overlook Your Employer

Many employers reimburse employees for taking college classes. Sometimes the course work must be directly related to the job. Other times, they pay for all classes leading to a degree. Some unions have negotiated for significant academic benefits so their members can increase their job skills. In any case, it is worth checking with your employer directly. Special arrangements might be made for you to take time off from work or to take your class right on your work site. Many larger companies bring classes to the work site with TV classes. You will not know if you do not ask.

Jobs On and Off Campus

Another source of funds is through student employment programs. More information will be found in chapter 10. There are many jobs available for students who need income. The main point is that many possibilities exist for helping college students get an education. Don't rule yourself out without checking. Inquire!

▐▐▐▶ NOTE: In the "Online Resources" section at the back of the book we have listed a few internet addresses that are sources of current information about financial aid.

⎍⎁⎍ Visit our website for additional financial resources and direct links to financial aid form applications. http://www.adultstudent.com/

Explore Your New Community

Remember what you do when you move into a new community? You explore. You don't passively sit and wait for someone to come knocking on your door with brochures about local businesses and services. Not at all. You go around visiting stores, businesses, and shopping centers in the area. You ask people for directions. You locate places that provide important services. You talk with neighbors to find out which places are best and which ones to avoid.

Starting college is like moving into a new community. The orientation leaders will give you stacks of information about college facilities and services available to you, but no matter how thorough they are, your own active exploring around campus will be more useful to you.

—✓— Our web site has a file listing support services and facilities available at most colleges. Use it as a basic checklist of places to visit: http://www.adultstudent.com/

If possible, visit every service or facility to get acquainted. Introduce yourself to staff members and ask what help they provide students. Don't be shy! All the college support services exist to help students like you succeed and graduate.

Make every effort to take the guided orientation tour provided by the college. The tour leader will answer many questions that all students have.

Be sure to pick up a copy of the college newspaper. It is free, and the first edition of the new school year will be loaded with information for new students.

Remember: The more quickly you become familiar with the college campus, the more quickly you will feel comfortable in this new community.

Locate Your Classrooms

Once you know which courses you will be taking, go find the rooms where each of your classes will meet. Learn where each classroom is located and how you'll get from one room to the next. The day classes start, trying to find your way around campus can be more hectic than a shopping mall the last weekend before Christmas!

Explore Your College

Take time to get acquainted with your school in the same way that you would be curious about a new community you move into. Be active and curious, not passive or timid. Learn about the many resources and services available to you. You will feel comfortable about coming to campus more quickly, and the more you locate and use resources, the more successful you will be.

⫸ REMEMBER: *The entire school exists to help you get the education you want!*

Action Review

❏ Have I read through the college catalog?

❏ Do I have specific courses in mind that I want to take?

❏ Have I found out if I need to apply for admission?

❏ Have I checked with the financial aid office to find out about my eligibility for financial assistance?

❏ Have I inquired about educational benefits or support from my employer?

❏ Do I know how to register for the courses I want?

❏ Do I know where my classrooms are located?

❏ Have I explored the campus to find out what is available to students?

❏ Do I feel well oriented to the college?

Support Group Activities

1. Talk about what difficulties you encountered trying to get registered for courses. Talk about the courses you plan to take. Help each other look into ways to tailor your selection of courses to fit your unique interests and needs. Be frank with each other about your financial needs. Someone in your group may know of a way to get extra financial help.

2. Plan a resources treasure hunt. Make up a list of places, offices, centers, and services you want to know about. Be sure to include the nearby neighborhood in your exploration. Find the location of stores, bank branches, the post office, copy centers, eating places, book stores, yogurt shops, and best pizza place. Split up into search teams. Divide up the list. Agree to meet at a certain place at a certain time. Afterwards talk with each other about what you found.

Chapter 4

How to Succeed in College

Can you describe how ordinary people succeed as college students?

Do you know what it means to view college as a learning environment?

Do you know how to take good lecture notes?

Can you explain the affect of self-esteem on success in college?

I'm a single parent, low-income, first generation student and a black female. I'm surely one that sociologists would label as disadvantaged. But with the assistance of the special services program and my desire, my commitment and strong will to distance myself from the labels and statistics, I have achieved my goal of completing college.

—Edna Mae Pitman
1989 TRIO Achiever Award Winner
(One of 26 college students in the nation selected by the National Council of Educational Opportunity Association from more than 425,000 students in TRIO programs.)

Success in Each Course Leads to Success in College

You can do well in college without being an ideal student. Success comes from being motivated to succeed and doing the things that lead to success in your courses. Thousands of ordinary people who are nervous, have doubts, and who didn't stand out in high school do very well in college.

Research into student success shows that students who do consistently well in the courses they take are those who:

+ find out at the first class meeting when all the tests will be held and when papers or projects are due.
+ attend all classes.
+ prepare for each class in advance.
+ ask several good questions during class.
+ take good lecture notes.
+ organize their time well.
+ study regularly.
+ set specific study goals each time they study.
+ hand in course work on time.
+ prepare for tests by writing practice tests.
+ stop studying when they reach their study goals.
+ work well with other students on group projects.

In addition, successful students are self-motivated, appreciate and encourage other students, have strong self-esteem and self-confidence, develop good study habits, and associate with other successful students. More about this later.

Find Out What is Required

Successful students actively determine the requirements for each course. During the first lecture they get answers to these key questions:

✦ Which chapters in the textbook will be covered?
✦ When will the exams be given?
✦ What material will each exam cover?
✦ What type of questions will be on the exams—essay, multiple choice?
✦ Are there past exams on file in the library?
✦ Will other work be required?
✦ When will the work be due?
✦ How will grades in the course be determined?
✦ What are the instructor's office hours? The location?
✦ Does the instructor have an outline of the most important terms and concepts to be covered?

These questions are a starting point. Others will occur as you go along. This is why having the phone number of another student in each of your classes can be very useful.

Many instructors provide a handout called a course syllabus. If you don't receive a handout, be sure to write everything down in your notebook. After class compare notes with other students.

Get Ready for the Avalanche:
The Smartest Way to Organize Your Notebooks

We suggest that you purchase a separate, three ring notebook for each course. Select a different color notebook for each one. This helps avoid the "Oh no! I can't believe I brought the wrong notebook today!" experience. Be sure to write your name, address, and phone number in each notebook.

Purchase notebooks that have at least five color tabbed sections: the first contains the course syllabus and any other instructions specific to the course; the second holds paper for your class notes; the third holds assignments ready to hand in;

the fourth holds assignments/tests handed back; the fifth includes extra handouts from your instructor.

How do you place all the handouts into a three ring notebook? Either purchase a small, inexpensive hole puncher or find the location of a three hole puncher you can use.

Organizing your course materials in this way will make it much easier to be a successful student. Reminder: *After going to all this trouble, be sure to take your notebook and a pen to each class!*

Take Good Lecture Notes

Getting a good grade in a course starts with taking good lecture notes. The nature of human memory is such that people soon forget most of what they hear no matter how much they intend to remember.

Several days after a lecture, most students can recall only a small percentage of what the instructor said. If you ask a student who doesn't take notes to tell you about some details about what the instructor said last week, you will quickly see how important note taking is for accurate recall. So, unless you tape record the lectures or trade note taking with a classmate, you need to take notes at every lecture.

Always take notes in the same notebook. Date each day's notes. Always follow the last lecture with notes from the next lecture. Do not mix lecture notes from different courses and different days in the same notebook.

Lectures are like textbook chapters. Each usually has a main theme and makes several important points supported by examples and/or facts. If you listen for them, they will be easier to hear.

Since teachers don't necessarily teach in a way that makes a single note-taking system workable, it is wise to have more than one way of taking notes. If the instructor is highly organized, the outline form for taking notes will work well.

⏦ You can read more about how to improve your listening skills by checking the Classroom Listening section of our web site: http://www.adultstudent.com/

Outline Format:

Outlining is the most traditional way of taking notes. Outlines work well for lectures or talks where the instructor is organized and presents ideas in a logical order. Outlines begin with a main topic. Major points are given similar headings (A, B, C, etc.) followed by supporting points (1, 2, etc.). The advantage of using an outline form is that points can continue to be broken down into more minor points. There are two disadvantages to outlining. First, an outline can't be done if the speaker isn't organized. Second, students often get so involved writing that it is easy to miss part of the information.

Summary Method:

A second method of note-taking is the summary method. This method works particularly well for auditory learners. In this method you will listen for several minutes, and then write a short paragraph summarizing the main points. This method is particularly useful when an instructor uses long examples or stories, or is disorganized. The trick is to be able to write a couple of good sentences or a short paragraph without losing the next topic being discussed. This system doesn't work well if there are lots of facts you need to write down. Don't bother writing facts that are in your text or on a handout, though.

Mapping:

A third method of note-taking is called mapping. Mapping is a highly visual method and works well for visual learners. Mapping begins with a clean sheet of paper. Each main idea is placed near the center of the paper as it is presented. Once written, draw a circle around each main idea. (Most lectures won't contain more than three or four main ideas.) As significant details are given they are placed on a line that branches off from the circle. Minor details will branch from the significant details. The advantages to this method are that it is brief, flexible, and fits either organized or disorganized lectures.

─⋀─ See our web site for Note-Taking Samples.

Are You An Active Learner?

It is important to learn how to take good notes because in college the responsibility for learning is the student's, not the teacher's. You cannot sit back passively and expect instructors to entertain you. It is not an instructor's responsibility to push you to learn or to make sure you get your assignments done, not like it may have been in high school. Succeeding in college is your responsibility, and that means being an active learner.

Are Your Goals Self-Chosen?

Success is to reach a goal. Successful students are students who choose and reach their goals. Getting to any goal you select and work for makes you successful.

The key is to make certain your goals are self-chosen. It is less motivating and less satisfying to have goals that others have selected for you.

> I got top grades. Mostly, it was because I attended all classes, and generally put a lot of time and effort into learning. However, I also made sure that every teacher knew my name by the end of the quarter. I always sat in the front of the room, and asked one or two intelligent questions during every class (the sort of question developed only by studying the class material outside of class). Once I felt that the professor recognized me as a student that cared about the material covered in the class, I made an appointment during office hours and pursued some other aspect of the course material with the professor. In this way, I was able to get the person to add a name to the face of the inquisitive and interested older student who sat in the front row. I'm sure that where my grade was borderline a couple of times, I was given the advantage because of the reputation I so carefully cultivated for myself. It couldn't have hurt.—MK

➤ If you do not have specific career goals or personal life goals, read the "Career Choice, Career Change" file at our web site now: http://www.adultstudent.com/

Also, talk with counselors in the careers center at your college. There is a wealth of helpful information available.

Good Study Habits Are Very Important

Your habits determine how much you learn during the time you spend studying. Two students may spend the same amount of time in classes and studying, but the student with good study habits learns more and gets a better education than the student with poor study habits. The chapters ahead will describe good study habits and show how you can develop them.

Enjoy Reading and Learning

Marion Drake, an instructor who works with adult students, says to buy a good dictionary and enjoy learning about the meanings of words. "We do best what we do most," she says, "so stop watching television. Spend lots of time reading." She says develop a passion for the subject and don't just memorize terms, learn what the concepts and principles mean.

Action Review: Checklist for Success

❑ Do I act in ways that lead to success in my courses?

❑ Do I have well organized course notebooks?

❑ Do I take good lecture notes?

❑ Am I an active learner?

Support Group Activity

Make up a your own lists describing successful and unsuccessful students. One of you write the lists down on a sheet of paper. On one list describe what a student can do to increase chances of succeeding. Then to provide contrast, make up a second list of what students do that reduces their chance of succeeding. Include what attitudes and habits you believe help or hinder success in college.

To get extra mileage from this activity, interview several adult students that you see as successful. Find out what they have to say about why they are successful. After you've talked with them discuss what you learned from them.

Note: If you write out a summary of your two lists for each other to have, please mail or e-mail us a copy. Our post office address is at the end of the book. Some students get very creative. The poem on the next page is what one student shared with us. It is reprinted here with her permission.

A Is For **Attitude**

The Alphabet of Success

A is for **Attitude**, it's where it all begins.
B is for **Believing** in yourself to the end.
C is for **Caring** enough to do your best.
D is **Doing** more than just passing the test.
E is for **Enjoying** the life that you live.
F is the **Future** rewards school will give.
G is for the **Goals** you plan to achieve.
H is for **Hanging-In-There** when tempted to leave.
I is for **Imagining** the things you can do.
J is for **Judging** the false from the true.
K is for **Knowledge** and nothing beats this.
L knows that **Labor** can be an abyss.
M is for **Mistakes** which we all make sometimes.
N is **Not Letting** them keep you behind.
O is the **Omnipotent** power we possess.
P is for **Plowing** the fields of success.
Q never **Quits** because that's defeat.
R stands for **Respect**, a two-sided treat.
S is for **Support** that we need to help us through.
T is for **Time Management** and for **Trying**, too.
U is **Understanding** how things should be done.
V knows the **Value** of having some fun.
W is the **Wisdom** to be the best you can.
X is a **variable**, like in algebra, man.
Y is **Your** choice to be something more.
Z is the **Zenith** we are all reaching for.

—*Lynn Reese*

Chapter 5

The Best Way to Study

Do you know how to create study schedules?

Do you know how to set study goals?

Do you work on high-priority items while ignoring less important matters?

Have you learned the most widely used and effective way to study?

Do you know that your studying time can be reduced by reading to answer questions?

Have you arranged a good study area for yourself?

Do you use principles of psychology on yourself when you study?

Start By Listing Your Study Goals

Study goals help you focus your time and energy. They help you take the step-by-step actions that lead to reaching your dream for a better future. Setting goals is one of the best ways to motivate yourself to study efficiently and effectively.

Students who don't set goals or schedule their time are usually uncertain about what to do from hour to hour. Students who identify what they should study to pass a course and create a schedule to achieve their study goals, usually succeed more easily than they imagined. Here's how to set study goals and design a schedule to achieve them.

Determine What Your Study Goals Should Be

First, you have to ask, "What do I have to do to pass the course?" In most courses you have to do the following:

+ Attend class.
+ Participate in class discussions.
+ Pass quizzes.
+ Write papers.
+ Pass tests.
+ Complete projects.

To set up a study schedule ask these questions:

1. When is each test, paper, or project due?
2. How can I space my studying so that I don't put everything off until the end?
3. How much should I do each day if I wish to accomplish everything on schedule?

Answering these questions will allow you to design an effective schedule for reaching your study goals. You will know what to do and know when you can stop!

How to Manage Your Time

Fill in Your Calendar

Your greatest aid will be a calendar with spaces that you can fill in with important dates and obligations. Obtain a big year-at-a-glance calendar or a monthly calendar that you can tear apart and pin up on your wall. You want to be able to see at a glance what is ahead for the entire term or semester.

Fill in dates when examinations are scheduled and when papers and projects are due. Fill in all the times that you plan to do things with your family, meetings, concerts, and other events.

Create Weekly Schedules

Once you have a picture of your major commitments for weeks and months ahead, you can make up a weekly schedule of your classes, study hours, work hours and other obligations. A weekly schedule organizes what you do with your time. It shows you the places where you have extra hours you can use for studying. A schedule decreases the amount of time you waste.

When making your schedule:

+ Budget some time to prepare for each class by reviewing notes and creating questions.
+ Designate time for personal responsibilities.
+ Reserve time to study course notes and write questions as soon as possible after each class.
+ Study difficult subjects when you will have the least interruptions.
+ Schedule time for your family and other important activities.

When you create a good time management/study schedule, it will motivate you. In fact, some students get so carried away we need to caution you to discipline yourself to stop studying! When you reach the scheduled time to stop, go get some exercise or do whatever you want to do. *Practice being a self-stopper!*

The problem for some students is that they study so much they use their time inefficiently. C. Northcoat Parkinson observed that "work expands to fill available time." You may have experienced this phenomenon. Let's say that you had in mind cleaning up the house or doing some yardwork during three hours available on Saturday morning. If you have three hours available, it will probably take you three hours to get the job done.

But let's say that before you start to work you learn that a very special person is coming by to visit and will arrive in about 30 minutes. You would probably be able to clean the house or mow the yard reasonably well in fewer than 30 minutes. What we suggest is that you decide what has to be done, do it, and then stop.

Time management experts often say that things not worth doing are not worth doing well. With less important jobs or matters don't waste precious time doing them as well as you can. Do them quickly, just good enough to get by. Use your precious time for more important things.

The main thing to accomplish is to control your activities rather than letting your activities control you!

A weekly time schedule that lets you fill in every half hour of the day, from early morning until late at night, will show you that you have many more hours each week than you might have ever realized. (Note: It will help your family if you post a copy where they can see it.)

Clocks and Success

See clocks as helpers, not op-pressors. The better you learn effective time management skills, the more you can get done in the little time you have available. Visualize clocks such as this old-fashioned, three-legged alarm clock as leading you over stacks of books to your diploma.

Remember, you need clocks and a good personal organizer when your dream for your future is to succeed in college and still have a life. Clocks are your friends!

Make Daily "To Do" Lists

Take a few minutes each evening to list the important things that you have to do the next day. List those things most important to be done, then plan ahead. Here's what one student reported doing:

> On a daily scale, I prepare myself by getting my book bag ready to go out the door the night before. I make sure I have paper, pens, books, calculator—everything I will need for the next day's classes. This saves much searching time and also reduces stress the next morning. Along with all the supplies I *will* need, I make sure there is nothing in my bag that I *won't* need. This includes extra books, note pads, tennis shoes, a broken door handle—anything just along for the ride.

Your "to do" list gives you a way to make decisions about what you do during the day. It reminds you what is important to do and what to say "no" to. It also lets you know when you are done.

Get in the habit of putting your time and energy into your highest priority items. Don't deceive yourself by thinking that you will get to the really big project after you get all the little things out of the way. What happens is that by the time you finish the little, unimportant tasks your time is gone and you are too tired to work on the important project. The same student quoted above says:

> To me the most important thing is *putting first things first*. A set study time is a priority. Once time is decided upon, decide what needs to be done and *do it*. One way I can remind myself of the importance of my commitments is to picture the result of my actions. I ask myself "How will watching TV instead of studying affect my future?" This puts things in perspective and reminds me of my priorities.

Your Study Area

The environment where you study affects how well you learn. Here are some tips about what to do and not do:

Study in the same place at home and at school. Don't keep changing your studying locations. New places distract you.

Create a study area for yourself at home. Do what you can to make it the place where your attention is devoted entirely to your studying. If you study at a desk, keep it cleared off.

Use a comfortable chair. It will be a good investment to get a comfortable chair that adjusts for height and back support. Discomfort can lead to muscle strain and physical distractions.

Arrange good lighting. To reduce eye strain, your room should be well lit, with the main light source off to one side. A light directly behind or in front of you will be reflected from the glossy pages of your textbooks. A constant glare tires your eyes more quickly than indirect lighting. If you can't shift the lamp, shift your desk. Place the desk so that no portion of the bulb shines directly into your eyes.

If you wear glasses, consider having them tinted slightly. Older eyes are vulnerable to eye strain.

> I loved my study area. My kids kept giving me posters to hang on the wall, and soon I felt that my corner was like the typical student's study area. Over my desk was my favorite "hunk" poster with him standing on the beach wearing shorts. He and I spent a lot of hours together, and I can still visualize that poster.—MK

Neutralize Noisy Distractions

Use steady background sounds to neutralize distracting noises. Play your radio or stereo system *softly* while you study to create a steady background of "white noise" to mask occasional sounds. Experiment with stations, tapes or CDs until you find what works best for you. Instrumental (non-vocal) music is usually best.

⏩ Don't try to study with the television on.

If you want to watch a TV program, then watch it. But don't try to avoid feeling guilty about watching television by having your book open to read during commercials. Studying with the TV set on is *academic suicide*. Use television time as a reward after you have completed a study period, if you wish.

The Big Picture

Every person who is both busy and effective makes decisions about what to do and what not to do with their time…

+ You started with your dream.
+ You decided that going to college was the way to reach your dream of a better life.
+ You confront your fears and concerns.
+ You select courses that lead to what you want out of college.
+ You imagine yourself succeeding in your courses.
+ You identify what you have to do to pass each course.
+ You develop monthly and weekly schedules for doing what it takes to complete course requirements.
+ You make "to do" lists that help you focus on your highest priority activities each day.
+ You stick with your daily schedule.
+ You balance being a self-starter with being a self-stopper.
+ You make a plan that leaves time for your family, your job, and other important activities.
+ You become very good at learning, passing tests, and getting high grades.

What Psychologists Know About Learning

Psychologists have studied how people learn for almost 100 years. You can use their research findings to improve your ability to learn and remember. Their research also helps show what interferes with learning and remembering.

Here are some important principles to understand:

✦ The weakest form of learning is *passive recognition*. Studying is not the same as reading your Sunday newspaper. Reading your textbook is not the same as reading a novel.

✦ The strongest form of learning is *active recall*. This learning method is to read the material with curiosity, intending to remember what you read, and then from memory write or verbally give a summary of what you learned. Passively reading your textbooks and lecture notes over and over again is no fun and is an inefficient way to learn.

✦ How well you first learn and then later recall what you study is influenced by your study environment, study plan, and learning style.

The purpose of any test is to measure what you have learned. This means that to pass tests you must start by learning the information you will be tested on!

Textbooks are not written to entertain you. When it comes to studying, you must use study techniques that motivate you to mentally reach out and grasp important information.

Have You Had Trouble Learning?

Your past experience in school may not have been the most positive. Perhaps you couldn't spell your way out of a paper bag and this turned you off from writing assignments. Maybe you reverse numbers and still have trouble with phone numbers and your checkbook. You can understand if you are told instructions, but not if you read them—or vice versa. You may have had a learning disability and never known it.

Sometimes the trouble you have with learning can be inherited. If your father or mother or grandparent had great difficulty spelling, you may have great difficulty spelling. Other times, difficulty in learning can be caused by an injury or illness. The Office of Disability or Counseling Office can help evaluate your difficulty and assist with tools to compensate. The American Disability Act 504 mandates schools provide the assistance you need to develop your potential. Figures for school children diagnosed with learning disabilities show a more than 250% increase since 1975. When you last went to school, learning disabilities may not have received adequate attention.

Tips received from those who have special needs are included in the acronym LEARNING:

L Let instructors know how they can help you.

E Expedite Extra time on written or oral tests.

A Art work and color coding 3x5 cards helps memory.

R Record lectures on cassette tape.

N Need to keep Noise and visual distractions to a minimum.

I Include tutorial help for difficult subjects.

N Notify administrators about problems you encounter.

G Get a computer with a spelling and Grammar checker.

Everyone has strengths and weaknesses in learning. The trick is to accentuate your strengths and shore up your weaknesses.

Remember, learning disability has nothing to do with intelligence. Einstein, Leonardo Da Vinci, Thomas Edison, Cher, and Tom Cruise are all known to have learning disabilities.

The Secret to Rapid Learning and Success in Classes: Ask and Answer Questions

The most effective learning technique is very simple. It is to develop the habit of reading textbooks, taking lecture notes and studying by asking and answering questions. When you do this you save many hours studying and have time to spend with your family, hold a job, take trips, attend concerts, and lead a balanced life.

Learning this study technique will take some effort because you will probably have to change some old reading habits. Such changes can be difficult. In the long run, however, the benefit is worth the effort, so stick with it.

How to Increase Your Studying Efficiency, Comprehension, and Ability to Remember

If you want to spend less time studying and remember better, focus on figuring out the important questions and the answers to them. The following steps will increase your learning speed, comprehension, and memory. Here is how to do it:

Skim Through Each Chapter Looking for Sources of Questions

You are sitting at your desk. The instructor has told you what chapters to study in the textbook. You open the textbook. Do you start reading the textbook as though it is a novel? No! Here is what to do:

First, look at the beginning of the chapter to see whether or not there are chapter objectives or a list of questions. Read them.

Second, look at the end of the chapter to see if there is a chapter summary. If so, read it right away! This is where you will find the important points the authors wish to stress.

IIII➤ When reading textbooks you decrease your study time by reading the chapter objectives and the summary at the end of the chapter before reading the chapter! (Quick test: Did you do that with this chapter?)

Third, skim through the chapter quickly. How do you skim a chapter? Glance through it rapidly the way you would look at a magazine that you are considering buying. You want a picture of the forest before you examine any trees. Look for titles, sub-titles, illustrations, pictures, charts, highlighted words or phrases, and statements that will give you a basic idea of what the chapter is about.

Fourth, skim the chapter a second time turning titles, sub-titles, and highlighted terms into questions. For instance, "Maslow's Hierarchy of Needs" is a section heading in a psychology textbook. When you see such a heading ask yourself "What is the hierarchy of needs that Maslow described?"

By asking questions about the material in the chapter, you alert yourself to the important points in the chapter. Reading in this manner is active rather than passive. When you ask questions, you will quickly develop a good sense of the questions the instructor will ask on tests.

What does a good question look like? It usually starts with a phrase like:

Name three kinds of…
_____ is an example of what?
Describe the ways that…
List the important points about…
The pioneering research was done by…
The early research proved…
What does _____ mean?
The definition of _____ is…
The three stages of development are…

Read to Answer Questions

Now it is time to read. Read fairly rapidly. Read to find the answers to questions you asked while skimming the chapter.

⫸ In many instances, your questions and answers will be in titles, subtitles, or lead sentences and chapter summaries.

As you read, if you come to the answer to material that raises a new question, slow down, ask and then answer the new question.

Write a Summary

After you read the chapter to answer your questions, close the book. Write a short summary of what you have just read. You learn best when you write a summary of the main points and facts from memory.

Recite What You Remember

If you commute in your own car or have a place where people will not be bothered by your talking out loud, a second way to learn course material rapidly is to verbalize what you have just read. Plan to take a few minutes skimming through the textbook before starting your commute. Then as you drive along, talk to yourself out loud about what you just learned.

The more sensory systems and muscles you involve in your learning the faster and more long lasting your learning will be. Talking to yourself shows you are study-smart!

Students who are not study-smart waste a lot of time by reading textbook chapters over and over without proving to themselves that they truly learned the contents of the chapter. They think, "I read it, I underlined it, I know what it's about." *Don't make that mistake!* Prove to yourself that you comprehend the chapter by answering questions out loud and writing chapter summaries.

IIII➤ Underlining or using a yellow highlighter will not lead to remembering nearly as well as writing or reciting what you know!

Make a List of Terms and Concepts
The fastest way to master a new subject is to focus on learning what the terms and concepts mean. To accomplish this quickly, make a list of words, terms, principles, and concepts that you will be expected to define, explain, describe, or understand.

Many students find that 3 x 5 cards are useful. You write the term, concept, or principle on one side of the card. On the reverse side you write out the definition or explanation. Then, when it is time to recite and review what you know, you look at the card and try to state or write from memory the definition written out on the other side.

Using 3 x 5 cards is handy because you can carry them around with you instead of your textbook. When you have a few minutes after lunch, on the bus, or while waiting for a class to start you can use the time to review your definitions.

IIII➤ You do not need long blocks of time to study. You can study for a few minutes any time, any place!

Some commuting students make cassette tapes listing important terms and concepts. They use the tapes to give themselves an oral quiz as they drive along.

Review Frequently

Frequent reviews help anchor your learning. With written summaries and 3 x 5 cards you can go over what you've learned at any time. And, as you will see in the next chapter, you are well prepared to write practice questions.

The Benefits

This study method is simple, saves time, and it works! You study for a limited time and then stop with a feeling of confidence that you know the material. You spend less time rereading chapters and doing other time-consuming study activities. This study method gives you the feeling that you've mastered the material. When you know you can answer questions correctly and make accurate summaries, you feel confident. Here is what one student wrote on an evaluation at the end of a course:

> When I read this chapter I thought "Oh, come on! It can't be that simple." But yes, Virginia, it is that simple. What a difference it has made! I was taking an economics course and getting nowhere...I started studying this way and was amazed at how much I retained. I've also found that the method of writing questions during lectures works well. It gives me a good idea of what is likely to show up on tests.

Some Difficulties With Skimming, Asking Questions, and Summarizing

Changing old reading habits is not easy. Especially if you are used to reading every word, and are trying not to miss something. You have to use your mind actively when you ask questions and write summaries. This takes more energy than passively reading printed pages. On the other hand, you learn so fast with this method you may feel that something is wrong because you are not having to study as much as you thought it would take to get good grades!

Train the Way Athletes Do

This method is similar to the way athletes prepare for competition. Imagine yourself agreeing to run in a ten kilometer race several months from now. You will run with friends and it is important for all of you to do well. To be at your best, would you loaf around until the last few days and then prepare by running day and night until the time of the race? No. You'd start now with a weekly schedule of jogging and running. A little bit of practice on a regular basis prepares you the best. The same approach is true for effective studying and remembering.

When you use these study techniques you can expect the following results:

+ The quality of your questions and answers will improve with practice.
+ The amount of time it takes you to ask questions and write good summaries will decrease.
+ You will be able to cover large amounts of material in far less time.
+ You will find that you think up the same questions that your instructors ask.
+ Your study periods will be shorter and you will feel comfortable stopping when your study goals have been reached.

Work With Your Concentration Span

Have you ever sat reading for awhile and then suddenly realized you didn't know what you just read? Discovered that your mind wasn't paying attention to what your eyes were reading? This is not an uncommon experience for students.

The problem is that while you can make yourself sit and read hour after hour, your mind will take a break when it needs one. You are human. The length of time you can make your mind concentrate on a subject is limited even if you can make your body sit at a desk for hours.

Are you a morning person? Set the alarm for 5 a.m. and study before the rest of the household is up and leave chores for evening when your brain is disengaging. Does nap time after work help you feel mentally alert and full of "get up and go?"

Or, can you get more done late into the night? If so, then go ahead and study until one or two in the morning. Select the time of day to study when your mental juices are most alert.

The way to make your study time more productive is to start with what you can do now and build on that. On the average, how long can you study before your mind slips off to something else? Twenty-five minutes? Ten minutes? Most students can concentrate on a textbook 10 to 15 minutes before starting to daydream.

➤ For more information see our web site for a file on Concentration: http://www.adultstudent.com/

Record Your Study Time Segments

The next time you study, write down the time you start. Notice how long you read the textbook before your mind starts to daydream, then write down how many minutes you were able to concentrate. Don't set any particular goals for yourself yet. You first have to find out what is the normal span of time that you can concentrate reading textbook materials before your mind starts wandering.

Let's say that your study log shows that your average concentration span is about twelve minutes. This is the typical length for most beginning students. Even as low as five minutes, does not mean that you have an Attention Deficit Disorder. Accept ten to twelve minutes as your current level. Don't be bothered or upset thinking that you can't control your mind. Focus instead on increasing your concentration span in small, reasonable amounts.

Take Mandatory Breaks

Set up a study schedule that fits your concentration span. Take a short stretch after each study segment and a long break about once an hour.

You will probably find the end of a study segment coming so quickly you will want to continue. *Don't continue without your break!* Keep your agreement with yourself. If you decide to take a stretch break after each short segment, then do so. *Do not allow yourself to study more than the allotted time.* Get up and stretch. Get a drink of water or step outside for a breath of fresh air or a hug from a loved one before starting the next study segment. The amount of self-confidence you develop from being in control of your mind and actions will probably surprise you.

Mix Study Subjects

Here are more principles of learning:

- ✦ When you learn one set of facts and then follow it with similar facts or material, the second set will interfere with your memory of the first and the first will interfere with your memory of the second.
- ✦ When you try to learn lots of information at one time you remember the first items and the last items best. The middle is most difficult to recall.

When Steve came into the learning center he was tired and discouraged. He worked full time, was enrolled in three night courses, and studied many hours evenings and weekends. As hard as he studied, however, he found it difficult to remember the material the way he felt he should.

Did Steve have a memory problem? No. His problem was that he would study one subject all evening or all morning and then switch to another subject the next day.

The more you try to learn similar material at one time, the worse your recall will be. How can you avoid this problem when you have lots of material to study? The best way is to mix your study hours with dissimilar material.

⫸ Do not devote one long study period to one subject.

Switch subjects about once an hour. Always try to make your new subject as different as possible from the subject you have just finished. That way your mind can be assimilating one topic while you are reading about another.

Principles of Learning in Action

Here is an example of a study schedule using the principles described above:

15 min.—history
    1 min. stretch break
15 min.—history
    1 min. stretch break
15 min.—history
    10 min. break—drink
    some water, walk the dog
15 min.—math
    1 min. stretch break
15 min.—math
    1 min. stretch break

15 min.—math
    10 min. break—drink fruit
    juice, make short
    phone call
15 min.—English
    1 min. stretch break
15 min.—English
    1 min. stretch break
15 min.—English
All done! Reward—watch
    video tape of *3rd Rock.*

Now that you know how to use the principles of learning to study efficiently and effectively, the next chapter will cover how to prepare for tests.

Action Review: Checklist for an Effective Study Plan

Use the following to rate how well you are doing at studying and following an effective learning plan:

❏ Do I have a calendar for the term marked with dates of all tests and assignments?

❏ Do I make weekly schedules of my classes and activities?

❏ Do I use daily "to do" lists?

❏ Can I do less important things quickly? Just good enough to get by?

❏ Do I set specific study goals for each course?

❏ Do I set up a schedule to achieve study goals?

❏ Do I follow my study goals schedule?

☐ Do I skim chapters first, ask questions, read the summaries, and then read to answer questions?

☐ Do I practice writing answers to questions and write chapter summaries?

☐ Do I make up lists of terms and concepts to use when I test my ability to recite definitions from memory?

☐ Have I created a good study area for myself?

☐ Do I study in short time periods and take breaks?

☐ Do I switch study subjects often?

☐ Do I stop studying when I said I would?

☐ Do I reward myself when I have successfully accomplished my study goals?

▮▮▶ Note: Re-do this checklist every three weeks to check your progress!

Support Group Activity

Show each other your schedules. Talk about your ways of managing your time well. Discuss how it feels to do so many things by the clock. Discuss what it feels like to be both a self-starter and a self-stopper. Share one thing that you do to just "get by" yet feel good about.

Talk with each other about your study habits. Find out what your study areas at home are like. Talk about how you handle distractions. Compliment each other for efforts and progress.

Chapter 6

How to Get
High Grades on Tests

Do you know that the best way to prepare for exams is to make and take practice tests?

Do you know that if you skip past a hard item during a test that you will often know the answer when you come back to it later?

Do you know that during an examination you can ask an instructor about test items?

Do you know that writing comments on tests is an effective way to reduce test anxiety?

How to Get High Grades on Tests

An examination is a series of questions you must answer. This means that your grades are determined by your ability to answer questions, not by how much the instructor likes you.

To get a high grade on a test you must be able to answer the questions asked by your instructor. That is why we emphasize looking for possible exam questions every time you read your textbook or course notes.

Do you see how this works? If you want to get high grades on your exams, spend your study time writing examination questions based on your textbook, class notes, and reading assignments. Then you take practice tests, ones that you created, covering predictable test items.

It is an inefficient use of your time to prepare for exams by reading, underlining, and rereading lecture notes and texts. No instructor conducts an exam by asking you to read your notes or textbook to him or her. Your instructors ask you to answer questions based on their lecture notes, readings, and the textbook. The point is obvious:

IIII➡ To do well on tests, devote your study time to
making and taking practice tests!

Make Practice Tests

Imagine that you are the instructor and have to write some questions that will test the class on the material covered. When you do this for each course you will be amazed at how close your test will match the one your instructor creates.

If you ever played an instrument in a concert or played on an athletic team you spent many hours rehearsing and practicing. Preparation for exams is the same. You prepare for exams by taking practice exams.

Write the Kind of Questions That Will Be On the Exam

What sorts of questions should you use? The same kind of

questions your instructor will ask. Remember what we said earlier, successful students begin a course asking *when* tests will be given and *what kind* they will be.

Will the test be multiple-choice? True-false? Short or long essay? A combination of these? Write your practice tests using the same kinds of questions.

Practicing the same kind of test items you will be required to answer in a test situation helps you relax. It builds your confidence. You feel less tension about tests. You know you have studied the right questions, and you sleep better knowing you've studied correctly.

Other Sources of Exam Questions

Textbooks and *lecture notes* are your best sources of questions, but there are other sources as well. They include the following:

Old Exams
You can look at past exams without feeling guilty. It is not cheating to do this. Old exams show you what an instructor thinks is the most important information students should know. Some school libraries keep a backlog of old tests on file.

By looking at old exams you may find out:

1. Does the instructor repeat favorite questions every year?
2. Do test questions come primarily from lecture notes, the text, or from a variety of sources?
3. Does the instructor prefer multiple-choice, short-answer, true-false, or essay questions?

Student Manuals
The student manual written to accompany a textbook is an excellent source of exam questions. Student manuals contain true-false, multiple-choice, fill-in, and short essay questions. Even if your exam will be made up of questions that differ in style, the manual questions are still valuable.

IIII▶ Note: *There may be a student manual for your textbook even if the instructor did not adopt it for the course.* Inquire about this. If a student manual exists, you can purchase it through the bookstore or directly from the publisher. It can be worth it's weight in gold!

Other Students

Fellow students can be an excellent source of test questions. You can talk with students who have taken the course in past semesters to get information about the types of questions to expect.

Your Instructor:

Don't overlook asking your instructor for information about subjects and topics emphasized on the exam. As we said earlier, most instructors are happy to tell you what material they think is especially important. Some instructors will let you look at old tests. It won't hurt to ask questions such as:

- ✦ Will the test be objective, essay, or fill in the blank? Will it be a short, 20-item, true-false quiz? A 60-item multiple-choice test? A long essay test?
- ✦ How much time will be allotted?
- ✦ What proportion of the test will be based on lecture, readings, and the textbook?

Create a Folder with Practice Tests

Start each course with a plan. Read ahead in the textbook before class. Take accurate lecture notes. Then as soon as possible, convert the information in your lecture notes and corresponding textbook chapters into questions.

Write your practice test questions on sheets of paper separate from your lecture notes. If you use 3x5 cards, place the question on one side and the answer on the other.

How to Quiz Yourself

1. Create a practice test from the questions you've been developing from textbook chapters, lecture notes, and other sources.
2. Take your practice test without referring to your books or notes. (Keep the answers hidden!)

3. If you are not sure of the answer to an item, try to guess. Make up answers as if you were in a real testing situation, trying to earn at least partial credit.
4. After you complete your practice test, check the accuracy of your answers.
5. Revise any test questions that need to be written differently.

This easy procedure lets you quiz yourself quickly. You look at your questions, give your answers, and then check to see if your answers were accurate.

Using your study time in this way creates a growing file of questions and answers that you are confident you could answer on an instructor's exam. When an exam is scheduled you don't have to pour over lecture notes and textbook chapters. Your folder of questions and answers or their stacks of question cards and quiz themselves. You could even show these to your instructor and get a view on how good your questions are.

Another way to take practice tests is to have a friend or family member quiz you. Later, when you feel ready, get together with several classmates and quiz each other.

Do you have to drive a distance to get to the college? Here's how one student takes advantage of the time in her car:

> Besides doing 3x5 cards I record the questions on cassette tapes. I do a lot of driving. I play the tapes while I'm in the car. Hearing a question and saying the answer out loud helps. When I record the tapes I put on enough questions to make up about 15 minutes. Then I record about 15 minutes of music, changing back and forth between the two. For me the best music has a lively beat and no words, Bolero, Angel's Crossing etc.

Practice Tests Reduce Test Anxiety in All Subjects

Making and taking practice tests will eliminate the need for last minute cramming and greatly reduce exam panic. Short practice tests, taken every several days, will let you master small amounts of information each week.

This method helps reduce anxiety in math and science courses. Success in every course comes from frequent self-testing on the kinds of items that will be on instructor's exams. This method creates a feeling of familiarity and mastery even on math and science quizzes.

Before a mid-term or final exam, compile a comprehensive practice test made up of sample questions from your weekly tests. You'll be pleasantly surprised at how much easier it is to pass your final practice test when you have been taking weekly tests.

IIII➤ Remember: To reduce test anxiety, keep taking practice tests!

The Advantages of Practice Tests

Predicting exam questions is the most useful technique you can use for learning the important concepts covered in your courses. As amazing as it may seem, students who write test questions and take weekly practice tests spend *less time studying and get better grades!*

You also remember what you learn much better than when you cram for exams. The research by psychologists shows that people remember material better when they review and rehearse it.

Some instructors will use test questions you write—especially well-written multiple choice or true-false items. It never hurts to ask the instructor if he or she would like to see questions you've written. Be sure to include chapter and page references, and mark the correct alternative. What a boost to sit down to a test and see *your* questions on it!—MK

The effectiveness of this study method has been proven over and over with thousands of students. This method helps you learn each subject quickly, get high grades, and obtain an excellent education. Your success in life is not determined by your course grades. It is a matter of what you know and what you can do. When you go to a dental hygienist to have your teeth cleaned, do you ask "What grades did you receive in school?" Probably not. You select professional services on the basis of what people know and can do.

How to Take Tests

General Guidelines

1. Read the instructions carefully. Glance at the entire exam to see where you'll earn the most points. Get a picture of how the test is laid out.
2. Look to see if answering questions that will be easy for you will earn as many points as the more difficult questions. If so, complete the easy questions first. After answering them you'll have more confidence, and you will be able to pass on to the more difficult questions. Do not start with the most difficult questions, get stuck on them, and then panic when you begin to run out of time.
3. Read each question carefully to grasp exactly what it is asking you to do. If the stem of the question says "What is an argument against...," then respond as requested. *Do exactly what the instructor requests!*
4. When you find an extremely difficult question or one you don't understand, move on to easier questions. Come back later to the ones you skipped. This reduces anxiety, saves time, and lets your subconscious mind search for the answer while you think about other items. Expect the answer to come to just as you do when trying to recall a person's name. Skipping past hard items is also practical because sometimes you find a clue to the answer in questions that follow.

Three Kinds of Tests

There are three kinds of tests: tests that require you to *recognize* the right answer, tests that require you to *recall* the right answer from memory and write it down, and tests that require you to *synthesize* the material you have been studying.

Recognition Tests

Multiple-choice, true-false, and matching items are tests of recognition.

▐▐▶ Tip: Many tests are given by using a scantron card for the answers. This makes grading the test easier but if you are in a hurry or under stress, it is easy to get on the wrong number for the answer. To avoid this problem use a ruler or straight edge of another paper to line your marked answers and check your number from time to time.

Read recognition questions carefully, but answer them quickly. If the answer is not immediately obvious to you, put a mark by the item and come back to it later. Never leave a question unanswered, unless there is a penalty for guessing.

You may have heard an instructor or some expert say to never change answers on a test. That is not good advice. Research shows that a much larger number of students gain by changing answers than the number of students who lose points by changing answers. Be careful, of course, about changing answers, but your second thought, *if you have prepared well*, has a good chance of being correct. After the tests are handed back, check to see how many times answers you changed were right.

Multiple-Choice Questions. When you answer a multiple-choice question, eliminate the incorrect alternatives first. This saves time and increases your chance of determining the right answer.

Pay close attention to key words and phrases such as "*According to* Freud…." or "Which is *not*…."

Go through the test rapidly, answering questions you know you know. Next, go back to those that you skipped the first time. Before handing in your exam go back to see if you read each item correctly. Be alert to questions that say "always, never, or only." There are few absolutes in life or on tests.

Additional Multiple-Choice Test Taking Tips:

✦ Put your name on the answer sheet!
✦ Read directions carefully before answering anything.
✦ When requested to choose the "best" answer, read them all very carefully.
✦ Read all options before answering.
✦ When undecided, read each answer with the question.
✦ Watch for clues to complete the sentence in the correct grammar.
✦ If you really do not have a clue, choose the longest answer.
✦ The second and third choices are more often correct than first and last choices.

Matching Questions. Read the directions for matching questions very carefully. If the instructions say "Match those that are opposite from each other," you'll kick yourself later if you matched similar items.

Identify the easy matches first. This reduces the chance of errors on more difficult matches.

IIII➤ Tip: Count the number of items in each column to see if they are equal. Cross off each item as you use it *unless* you may use it more than once.

True-False Questions. Don't waste time puzzling over true-false questions. They are usually the first items on a test with different kinds of recognition questions. Unfortunately, some students waste lots of time on several true-false questions. If an answer isn't obvious, move on to other questions. One or two true-false items aren't worth that many points. Besides, the answer may become apparent later in the test as you answer other items.

IIII➤ Tip: True/False tests frequently have more true answers than false. Unless you are penalized for incorrect answers, guess. *Do not leave blanks.* You have a 50/50 chance of being right.

Recall Tests

There are three types of tests of recall: long essays, short written answers, and fill-in items.

▐▶ If an instructor says it is a *blue book* examination, you must go to the bookstore and purchase a thin book filled with lined pages that has a blue cover. It was designed specifically for essay examinations.

Long Essay Questions. Take a little time to outline your essay before you start writing. When you have made sure you will cover the most important points you will be more confident and relaxed. Remember that the purpose of the essay is to demonstrate your knowledge and understanding.

A well-written essay usually includes the following:

1. **Introduction.** Briefly describe the most important questions or present the main issues. Tell the reader what you are going to say and why.
2. **Use headings and subheadings.** Use headings for each major point or issue. Use subheadings every few paragraphs. Subheadings give the reader a quick understanding of the way you have organized your answer. (Notice how the headings and subheadings in this chapter show how the information is organized.)
3. **Demonstrate Critical Thinking.** Every field has conflicting views, findings, and interpretations. Your ability to present conflicting views demonstrates a much higher level of mastery and critical thinking about a subject. If your life experience gives you reservations about major views in the field, then say so.
4. **Give examples.** Illustrate your points with examples. They demonstrate that you really know what you are taking about.
5. **Provide Definitions** Show that you know what a term or concept means by giving its definition. Remember, the purpose of the test is for you to demonstrate depth of learning.
6. **Summarize.** Tell the reader what you have said. Be careful,

however, to not include any new examples or information in the summary.

7. **Edit for clarity.** After you have finished writing, look through your essay to make certain you answered the important questions. Look for careless mistakes. Edit your answers and clarify your statements.

IIII➡ Note: To get yourself started on an essay question, it can help to ask yourself what are the important social, historical, psychological, economic, or physical aspects of this question.

Short-Answer Tests. A short answer test given during a typical 50 minute class period may contain from 20 to 40 items. Such tests usually say to:

◆ Summarize the main findings of....
◆ Define the terms and concepts listed below.
◆ State the main criticisms against....
◆ Identify the parts in the picture:
◆ Briefly describe two arguments in favor of....
◆ List the factors leading up to....
◆ Name the basic steps to follow in....
◆ Explain why....

Your answers on short-answer tests will usually be phrases and incomplete sentences. You will not be asked to write long paragraphs so do not study that way. The instructor wants an easy to read list of phrases and brief statements.

IIII➡ A helpful tip: Before you start writing answers, write some of the information you memorized on the back of the exam.

Synthesis Tests

Some instructors will give "open book" or "take-home" tests. An open book test is given in the classroom during the testing period. You will be allowed to use your text book and notes when answering questions. You will be expected to connect–or synthesize–two or more ideas into your answers. Since there is no one correct answer, the way you combine concepts and add support to what you say will be the basis for evaluation.

Take-home exams work in much the same way as open book exams with the main difference being the amount of time you have to answer the questions. Often, you will be given the exam questions at one class period and will come back with your answers at the next class period. This means that if your class meets once a week you will have a week to work on your answers.

When Questions Puzzle You

What can you do with a question that stumps you? Skip it until the end of the test. While answering other items, you will probably recall some information related to the answer. Before turning in your exam write down *anything* that demonstrates some learning. Do not leave an answer blank. It gives an instructor a negative impression. If you can't figure out the exact answer, you can probably come close.

Nervous? Write Comments About the Test

If your heart is pounding, your palms sweating, and you start to feel overwhelmed, imagine the following statement at the top of the test: "Feel free to write comments about the test items."

Research by psychologist Wilbert J. McKeachie, an expert on teaching and learning, discovered that students who received examinations with the "Feel free to write comments...." statement printed at the top of tests, did better on the test than students who did not. He found that it did not matter if students actually wrote anything about the test or not! The mere presence of the statement improved the scores of many students. This means that if you feel anxious or nervous or have fears of failing, it will help to write comments in the side or back of the test.

You Can Ask Questions During the Exam

Exam questions are not always clear. Instructors know that. Many times they create exam questions in a hurry late at night and sometimes a question is not worded well. That is why many instructors will talk with you about a test question during the exam.

If, even though you studied well, there is still a question you don't understand, go up to the instructor and ask about it. Say "I don't remember this material from the lecture or the text. Where was this information presented?" Or, "there are several correct answers to this item, which one do you want?"

You have nothing to lose by asking for some hints. The instructor will not give you the answer, but may remind you where the information was located in the textbook.

What You Gain From These Test-Taking Methods

Students who use the methods described in this chapter:

+ usually receive high grades on tests.
+ earn more points for answers than predicted.
+ feel confident and relaxed during tests.
+ seldom leave out important information.
+ complete exams in time available.
+ seldom misread the test questions or answer questions incorrectly.
+ do not waste time on questions that stump them.
+ do not put wrong or irrelevant information in answers.
+ get more points on written items that let them "pad" their answers.
+ seldom develop exam panic.
+ get higher grades in their courses.
+ demonstrate to the instructor that they have mastered the course content.
+ sleep well the night before the exam!

Action Review: Checklist for Success in Preparing for and Taking Tests

❑ At the start of each course do I find out what kind of examination the instructor will use?

❑ After each class do I write and then quiz myself on possible test questions?

❑ Do I practice taking the tests I create every week?

❑ When I take tests, do I use the methods recommended in this chapter?

Support Group Activity

Talk with each other about taking tests. How do you feel and what do you do the night before? Do you feel confident? Get a good night's sleep? How do you feel on the way to the test? What is your self-talk like when you walk into the room and sit waiting for the tests to be passed out? Is taking tests similar to other life experiences you have had? Share practical tips with each other about what you do to handle your nervousness about tests

After you have taken tests, show each other the test results. Talk about how well you handled yourself and what you could do better next time. Compare the practice exams that you made up with the actual test. Find out if you were on target or not. Your study buddies will tell you!

Chapter 7

How to Write Excellent Papers

Do you know your starting point when writing papers should be, "What questions am I trying to answer in this paper?"

Do you know the ability to write excellent papers may depend on how well you know how to use the library?

Do you know which librarian to talk to when you need help?

Do you know the difference between a barely acceptable paper and an excellent one is determined by your ability to revise and rewrite?

The Secret to Writing "A" Papers

You do not have to have a high IQ to write a term paper that gets an "A." All you have to do is:

- ✦ always keep in mind you are writing your paper for one person, your instructor.
- ✦ select a topic interesting for you and one that your instructor feels is important.
- ✦ make your paper a series of answers to important questions.
- ✦ present contrasting views or positions to demonstrate your capacity for critical thinking.
- ✦ show your instructor your outline for your paper before putting a lot of work into it.

Interview Your Instructor

Select two potential topics for your paper. A good way to investigate a research topic is to consult an encyclopedia. The *Encyclopedia Britannica* is an excellent resource. If it covers a subject, it will provide you with a comprehensive summary and the important viewpoints about it.

Make a list of important questions and issues for each topic. Work up a one page outline of what you would do with each topic.

Meet with your instructor before you start writing your paper. Interview the instructor to find out which topic the instructor feels would be the best one for you to write about. Ask the instructor if there are important references you should look at and refer to in the paper. Ask the instructor "What important questions and critical issues should I cover in the paper?" Listen well. The instructor will probably tell you exactly what he or she will want to see in the paper. You make things much easier for yourself when you do this!

Start With Questions

Begin your research by listing specific questions you intend to answer in your paper. If you aren't certain how to start, go to the library and talk to one of the reference librarians. They can help you find sources of information you don't know about. That is what their job is. Use their expertise.

The Computer Can Do Your Search

Once you have a list of questions, start looking for answers. Begin in the college library. In most college libraries your search for information sources will start with a computer terminal. Catalogs are now online, and the old card catalog or microfiche are rapidly becoming tools of the pre-computer age. The online computer system records availability of books and journals and even allows you to reserve materials that are in other locations. If you are unsure of how to use the computer terminals, ask the librarian for help. The one thing that has not changed is that the librarian is a very helpful person.

Libraries have their index on computers and you can access information by author, subject, and title. You'll probably want to start with the subject index.

Use your imagination when searching the subject index. Look under every topic you can think of. The abstracts of articles are a quick way to research relevant data. Make notes of book titles and authors, and always write down the complete call number of the book. The *call number* is the library's code number that tells you exactly where the book is shelved.

IIII➡ Note: When you see the statement "reserve" or "reserve desk" by a book, you will *not* find the book in the open shelves. An instructor has had the book placed in a special reserve section where it can be signed out for a limited amount of time, usually a couple of hours to overnight.

Periodical Sources

The most recent information on a subject appears in professional journals long before it is written up in books. Look in the library's periodical index for titles of journals that would contain articles related to your topic.

Many college libraries have courses that teach you how to search for periodical information and write a research paper.

Be sure to look under "Journal," "American," and "National" in the alphabetical listings. The journals of professional groups are often titled *The Journal of...*, *The American...*, or *National Society of...*, etc.

When you write down call numbers for books and journals, you will notice that the books and journals with information about your topic will be located in two or three places in the library. Then when you go to these locations in the stacks, you will discover other useful books and journals.

From the journal articles you learn about books to research. From the books you will learn about journals that focus on your topic most frequently.

Skim articles and books first to get a general orientation. When you find useful data or passages you may want to quote in your paper, record the name and date of the publication, the title of the article or chapter, and write down or photocopy the quote exactly as it was printed. It is very frustrating when you can't remember which author you quoted or which statement in your notes is your own summary. Libraries have photocopiers available. You will save time using them.

Be sure to look at *The Reader's Guide to Periodical Literature.* It lists articles published in popular magazines. Don't discount magazines as a source of information, because some scientific research is published directly in them. Besides, the information is less technical than in professional journals and books.

If you do not find the information you need in your library, your librarian can search local, national and even international sources on the information highway to obtain for you the most up-to-date references. You may also find the information online through your own searching. When using periodical databases, it is now possible to e-mail the article or abstract to an e-mail address of your choice. You no longer have to print articles you want to look at further. You can just send them to yourself.

▐▐▐▶ Note: Libraries have greatly expanded their video and audio selections. If you find you learn easier by watching and listening, consider using these convenient resources.

Search for Answers

You'll discover that by having questions in mind that you want to answer, you can quickly cut through the massive amount of material that could otherwise distract you. By reading to answer your questions, you avoid the needless loss of hours wondering how much you should include in your paper.

Expect New Questions

In the process of answering questions, new questions may arise. You may find that as you do your research you need to change the original questions in some way or add some new ones.

Writing a Rough Draft

Now that you've gathered your information, it is time to write a rough draft about your questions and the answers you found. Write your first draft quickly. Don't waste time trying to make your first draft your final draft.

Start by presenting your questions and explaining why they are important.

Write the answers to each question. Make your point and back it up with examples. Answers to questions are more believable when they are clear and well supported.

Quote from your sources. Brief quotes, paraphrases, facts, and figures have more effect than personal impressions, opinions, or generalizations. Give exact references for your quotes, paraphrases and facts.

Arrange your answers so that they connect in a logical way. Connect them by saying, showing, explaining, or demonstrating how they are related to each other.

Demonstrate Critical Thinking

Very few instructors want you to parrot back exactly what some authority has said. They want you to show that you can think intelligently about the subject. They want you to demonstrate critical thinking.

How do you show critical thinking? By presenting contrasting or conflicting perspectives. Don't pick one viewpoint and present it as right while others are wrong. Present the strengths and weaknesses of one perspective and the strengths and weaknesses of a contrasting perspective.

Your life experience gives you an advantage over younger students here. You know there are always two sides to a story. Present both sides plus your own ideas about what this all means.

Summarize and Draw Conclusions

At the end of your paper summarize the main points and add two or three conclusions. The summary explains what you have done in your paper, justifies your conclusions, and demonstrates critical thinking. Be sure to check your summary against the introduction to your paper. Do they match? If not, revise your introduction.

Listen to Your Paper

The best way to quickly determine if your paper makes sense is to read it out loud. When you read it aloud, a rough sentence structure or a statement that does not make sense will be very apparent. After reading your paper aloud to yourself, consider reading it aloud to a study buddy or a classmate.

Correct Your Grammar and Spelling

Make sure that your spelling and grammar are accurate. Use a spell checker or a dictionary when in doubt. Have someone else proofread your paper. Few things bother instructors more than poor spelling and bad grammar. Instructors tend to give higher grades to papers clearly typed, grammatically correct, and free of spelling errors.

Consult Your Instructor

Make an appointment to go over your first draft with your instructor. Many instructors will give you good feedback about revising you will need to do if you want an "A."

Revise and Rewrite

The real writing of any paper, of course, takes place when you rewrite and edit your first draft. Most good papers require several revisions before achieving the final version.

During your rewriting, revising, and editing ask yourself:

+ Have I clearly stated the questions my paper will answer?
+ Are the questions I selected important to the topic and cover it well?
+ Have I answered the questions effectively?
+ Is my writing interesting to listen to?
+ Have I corrected grammatical, punctuation, and spelling errors?
+ Does my summary accurately cover the main points of my paper?
+ Do my conclusions demonstrate critical thinking and cover what I learned in the process of writing the paper?

> Note: If you feel the need for help with your writing, contact the English department. English departments usually run a writing skills center for non-English majors. It is worth looking into.

Caution: Do Not Cheat Or Plagiarize

According to a poll of 1000 college students conducted by *U.S. News & World Report* in 1999, 84% of the students said they believe they need to cheat to get ahead. Most of the cheating is to copy homework or purchase term papers from web sites. Some students cheat on exams with cell phones and pager messages.

Some students saw nothing wrong with copying passages from a book or magazine article and turning in the paper as his or her own work. They rationalize their actions as having too much pressure to do too much work and feeling that their career opportunities require them to get high grades using any means that they can.

Trying to pass off someone else's work as your own is called *plagiarism*. It is a form of lying. There are many negative consequences. You can be flunked if you are caught. Even if you succeed, you subvert your self-confidence when you face real-life career challenges. Plagiarism also diminishes your opinion of your instructors if you get away with it.

Colleges are taking steps, by-the-way, to deal with the problem of plagiarized term papers. The web site *www.plagiarism.org* supplies a high-powered program that can detect plagiarism in a paper.

It is human to consider taking shortcuts, but plagiarizing is not worth the risk. Plagiarism is unethical and usually illegal.

▐▐▶ It is plagiarism to turn in a paper written by another student. This means you don't let a study buddy copy your work, you don't copy theirs, and you don't do their work for them.

Make Your Papers Look Good

If you want a top grade, produce a clean, sharp looking paper. Type or word process all your papers. Instructors prefer printed, easy to read papers because of their constant struggle to avoid eye strain. If you don't have keyboard skills, consider taking a class. It is one of the best self-improvement efforts you can make.

Many English departments have their composition courses conducted as computer labs, so you might want to take an English composition course right away. It is a good way to develop computer literacy if you are not familiar with computers.

Make your paper as professional looking as possible. Most instructors will accept papers printed by dot matrix printers if the ribbon is not too old. Use clean white paper. Double space the lines. Keep handwritten corrections on the final copy at a minimum.

Be sure to follow all directions your instructor gives for the way you should do footnotes, references, and other procedures. It is a waste of time and energy to devote hours to a paper only to have it returned as incomplete. *The consequences of failing to follow directions can be costly.*

A word to the wise: Hand in a paper you are proud of! If it were a business report that would affect your chances for a pay increase, would you submit it the same way?

⏵ Note: *Always* make a copy of your paper. The original could get damaged or lost. Play it safe. Keep a copy and be sure it is saved on a computer disk.

How to Calculate Your Grade Point Average

You will probably learn about your grade in each course before the college sends you your grade report. If you don't want to wait, here is the method used for converting your course grades into a number called the Grade Point Average:

A = 4 grade points for each course hour
B = 3 grade points for each course hour
C = 2 grade points for each course hour
D = 1 grade point for each course hour
F = no points

To calculate your GPA, list how many credit hours each course was worth and the grade for each course. Multiply the credit hours for each course by the grade's value. Then add up both columns and divide the grade points by the credit hours:

Course	Credit Hours	Grade	Grade Point
Psychology	3	C	2 x 3 = 6
English	3	A	4 x 3 = 12
Biology	4	B	3 x 4 = 12
History	3	B	3 x 3 = 9
	13 hours		grade points = 39

Grade Point Average = 39 ÷ 13 = 3.0

Each term you add the new total of all your college credit hours and divide that number by the total of all your college grade points. By the end of your second year, for example, what would your GPA be if you had taken 120 credit hours and earned 420 grade points?

Action Review: Checklist for Success in Writing Papers and Using Your Library

❏ Do I write papers using the question and answer format?

❏ Have I asked the reference librarian for suggestions about where to look for information?

❏ Do I use the card catalog, microfiche, or online system to track down good reference sources?

❏ Do I get up-to-date information from professional journals?

❏ Are my quotes and references accurate?

❏ When my first draft is completed, do I ask the instructor to look it over and give me suggestions for improvement?

❏ Do I check for correct grammar and spelling?

❏ Do my papers reflect my ability for critical thinking?

❏ Am I proud of what I hand in?

Support Group Activity

Talk about what you know about your college library. What tips do you have for each other about using the online system? If none of you know, then arrange for a demonstration by one of the librarians.

When you are developing ideas for papers, bounce topic ideas and key questions back and forth. Choose topics that interest you. It helps to feel enthusiastic about your topic.

After you have produced your first rough draft, show it to the others. Read each other's papers out loud and ask questions. Help each other create contrasting perspectives that demonstrate critical thinking. Take turns giving each other both suggestions and appreciation.

REVIEW AND PREVIEW

The first seven chapters of this book covered basic information on how to get started in college and how to succeed in your courses. By now you have learned that your college provides helpful services and assistance on each of the areas covered in the first seven chapters. If you find yourself struggling with any of these challenges go to talk to someone in the college counseling department. The people there are friendly and very good at problem solving student difficulties. They will help you stick with your education plan.

The previous chapters covered important academic skills, the rest of the book covers important life skills. Without good life skills, you reduce your chances of getting the education you desire and the career you seek.

In some classes, for example, you will be required to team up with a few other students to do a project. Part of your grade will be based on how well your team does. As a member of a learning team, as with a work place team, you must deal with differences in personalities, working styles, and cultural backgrounds. In the next section you will find guidelines for understanding and successfully resolving predictable conflicts with others.

Do you handle pressure and constant change well? Select and transition into a new career easily? Enjoy working for an employer that does not provide job descriptions? Are you flexible and resilient? The final chapters show how to develop the inner strengths needed for thriving in a world of non-stop change.

Chapter 8

Learning Styles and Teaching Styles: How to Influence Instructors

Do you know that difficulties in a course can stem from a conflict between a student's learning style and the instructor's teaching style?

Do you know that college instructors do not have to take any classes on how to teach?

Do you know how to improve the teaching you get?

Do you know it is possible to overcome a poor start in a course and get a good final grade?

Learning Styles: They Can Help or Hinder

No matter how good a student you are, you will take courses from instructors who don't teach the way you learn. Research into why some students do well with one instructor but not another, uncovered a simple truth about academic life:

> *The way an instructor teaches will not fit with the way some students learn.*

Research findings and experience have identified the following important differences in how people learn.

External versus Internal Learning Styles

Psychologists have done extensive research on an important personality difference between people. It is called the "external and internal locus of control."

Externally oriented students believe information when it comes from an authority or expert. Information or suggestions from other sources aren't trusted as accurate.

If your instructor enjoys being an expert who tells the class exactly what to learn, the better an externally orientated student will do with this type of instructor. If you desire clear guidelines from an instructor, but take a course from someone who provides little direction, you may flounder.

Some students who want to listen to an authority react negatively to classes where the instructor encourages discussion and encourages students to develop their own views and answers. These students protest, "I didn't pay good money to sit and listen to a bunch of uninformed people express their opinions. I can get that in the cafeteria." This attitude is legitimate, but it is also narrow-minded.

The word *education* means to "draw out of." It does not mean "shovel into." A good education does not give you a diploma for learning how to seek out an expert for any question you have. A good education teaches you to think for yourself. It teaches you to ask questions and how to find the answers on your own.

Self-motivated, internally oriented students appreciate an instructor who allows them freedom to follow their own paths. Such students get upset with instructors who tell them exactly what they must learn, and in what way. For them, too much course structure is abrasive. They feel handicapped more than helped. Such reactions are legitimate and narrow minded.

Being Both Internal and External in Learning

Students who get the most out of school are able to follow the tightly-controlled steps used by some teachers and, at the same time, organize their own learning experiences when in a class taught by someone who gives few guidelines. Can you do both?

Auditory versus Visual Styles

Have you ever noticed that you can tell a person something but it doesn't register unless you write it down for them? Or that someone might read a note you've left, but the message didn't get through to their brain? That is because people differ in how information gets into their consciousness.

Some people learn best by reading. They must see something in writing before they believe it and remember it. Other people learn best by listening. Information doesn't stick well unless they hear it. What is your natural style?

- ✦ Do you prefer to listen to the radio or read newspapers for the news?
- ✦ Do you remember what you read the best or what is said to you?
- ✦ Would you rather read what an expert has written on a subject or hear the expert talk?

Based on your answers to these questions, which learning style do you tend to prefer? Auditory or visual?

Everyone learns by each way, of course. It is not an either/ or situation. Yet the differences between people are sometimes extreme enough to cause problems. If you have a visual learning style, you operate mainly on the basis of what you read. You may have difficulty with an instructor who believes that telling students what they should know is sufficient.

Visual Learning Style

If you learn best visually, you may be in trouble with an instructor who doesn't use handouts, emphasizes class discussion, and doesn't write much on the blackboard. The solution with a verbally oriented instructor is to:

1. Take good notes on what the instructor and your classmates say. After class fill in sentences and compare notes with other students.

2. Ask the instructor for suggested articles or books that will let you read the information you need to understand better.

3. Consciously work at listening and remembering what the instructor says. TIP: One woman wrote to us saying that she types her lecture notes immediately after every class.

4. If you are confused about a point, ask the instructor to tell you again and write down what you hear.

5. Ask instructor if an outline of the lecture is available.

Auditory Learning Style

If you have an auditory style, you will probably do well with an instructor who says everything to learn and do. You may have difficulty with a visually-oriented instructor. Such an instructor hands out a written statement about what to do to pass the course without discussing it, and assigns textbook material and outside readings that are never discussed in class.

The solution, if you have an auditory style in a class taught by a visually-oriented instructor is to:

1. Find classmates who will tell you what they learned from the textbook readings.

2. Dictate the main points from the reading assignments and handouts onto cassette tape and then listen to the tapes.

3. Consciously work at improving your ability to acquire information visually. (Note: For professional help, go to the reading improvement center or the office of disabilities.)

Understanding Differences in Temperament

Isabel Myers and her mother, Katheryn Briggs, developed a test to measure four dimensions of temperament identified by Carl Jung. Myers-Briggs type tests are probably the most popular personality tests given these days because of many benefits gained from seeing how differences in temperament explain misunderstandings between people.

This means that differences in *how* you and an instructor think are more important than differences in *what* you think. Here is how the four temperaments influence your learning style:

Extroversion versus Introversion

Instructors and students vary widely in how friendly they want to be and how much emotional distance they need to have. A friendly, extroverted instructor enjoys after-class contact with students. He or she may ask groups of students to meet and talk after class. If you are naturally friendly, you will have a great year.

If you are a more introverted person, however, you may suffer from too much personal attention and closeness. You would much rather have a quiet, more distant instructor who respects your need to be left alone. You like taking courses on the internet better than courses where you have to be part of a learning team with other students.

On the other hand, if you are an extroverted person with a more introverted instructor, you may find it puzzling to have him or her pulling away from you after class. After all, what are instructors for if not to be available for students? Yet your desire to be friendly may cause the instructor to stare at you and make excuses to get away. After that, you may feel avoided.

When it come to studying, the introverted person needs a private, quiet place where everyone stays away. The extroverted person likes to study in the kitchen, in a student lounge, or with classmates. If you grew up in a large family you may study best in a noisy place with lots of people around. Experiment with locations to see what works best for you. Don't hesitate to tell friends, relatives, and classmates with temperaments different than yours what you need.

Thinking versus Feeling

Descriptions of this dimension of temperament match up closely with left-brain/right-brain research findings. The left brain is where the speech center develops in most humans. The left brain is where you remember words, use logic, and think analytically. It gives you your ability to think rationally and unemotionally. The left brain thinks in a linear fashion. It is time oriented.

The right brain carries your memory for music. You think visually, emotionally, and irrationally in the right brain. It is the source of creativity and intuition. Right-brain thinking follows emotional logic. Using it, you think in patterns and jump from one spot in a pattern to another without apparent connection.

If you tend to be left-brained, you will be well matched to an instructor who gives you thorough, unemotional listings of facts, data, analytic explorations, hypotheses, logic, evidence, numbers, definition of terms, and rational conclusions.

If you tend to be left-brained and get an instructor who teaches in a right-brained way, you may find the course to be a bewildering experience. You may experience the instructor as weird, too emotional, disorganized, and a bit nutty.

If you tend to be right-brained with a left-brained teacher, the course will be painful for you. You'll feel like a thirsty person handed a glass of water only to find it is filled with sand.

||||▶ To resolve personality conflicts such as these, avoid indulging in the attitude "If only other people would change, my world would be a better place for me."

When you have a mismatch, try to find someone (perhaps even the instructor) who will translate the material into a form you understand better. More important, however, make an effort to gain more use of your other brain.

The situation may not be easy at first, but it gives you a chance to add another dimension to yourself. And isn't this why you're in school?

You do not have to give up your more natural and preferred way of thinking, feeling, and talking. What you can do is add more to what you already have. We'll get into more of this in the chapter on resiliency.

Sensation versus Intuition

Sensation oriented people are guided by experience. Intuitive people like fantasy, they are creative dreamers. According to David Keirsey and Marylin Bates, authors of *Please Understand Me*, differences on this dimension cause the widest gulf between people.

The sensation oriented student is practical, wanting facts and evidence. An intuitive instructor can fill the lecture hour with hypothetical explanations, theories, concepts, and a long list of views held by others.

A sensation oriented instructor gives practical instructions on what to do. An intuitive student wants to know what the underlying theories and concepts are, and asks "but what if?"

What to do about this sort of conflict? Stretch your understanding. Ask for what you need. Try to minimize the judging dimension of the next pair of traits.

Judging versus Perceiving

Judging people make up their minds quickly. They see people, viewpoints, and situations as good or bad, right or wrong.

The perceiving style is to observe without judgment. Such people can watch world events, movies, and hear opposing viewpoints without taking sides or having an opinion.

A judgmental style instructor believes there is a right way to think about the material, that contrary positions are wrong. This instructor may be openly critical of a theory that he or she doesn't like.

A perceiving instructor presents different positions without indicating that any of them are right or wrong. "On the other hand," is a favorite phrase. This instructor is frustrating for a judging style student who wants to know which way to think about something.

IIII➤ Note: If you want to take a Myers-Briggs type assessment of temperaments, check with the counseling office or careers center. Many colleges have a software program that lets you take the test and get a printout of your scores.

Learn to Appreciate Human Differences

We humans are all born with different temperaments and different ways of functioning in life. That is simply the way things work. When you experience conflicts with others at school, at work, or in your family, question your attitudes about other people. If you experience an irritating difference, use that as an opportunity to learn more about human nature. You might as well, because you won't change other people by complaining and criticizing them!

The better you know yourself, the more skillfully you will manage your learning style and the easier it will be to succeed in college!

Coping With Poor Teaching

You've had enough experience to know that every occupation has a few people who are excellent, many who are competent, and some who are poor at their craft. Don't be surprised when you discover that the same principle is true of college instructors. You will have a few who are outstanding, many who are very good, and a few who make you wonder how they keep their jobs.

A fact of college life is that college instructors can hold teaching positions without ever taking classes on how to teach. They do not have to be certified to teach, not like elementary and high school teachers. At the college level the responsibility for learning is on the student, not on the teacher. College students are expected to learn what the course covers, no matter how deficient in teaching skills the instructor is.

In 1998, seven-hundred students at the University of Wisconsin were asked to list what annoyed them most about their professors' way of teaching. The ratings were collected anonymously and covered all courses in all subjects. The complaints listed by the Wisconsin students were similar to student complaints at many colleges:

- Poor course organization, poor planning, important material rushed at the end.
- Too many films and videos shown, often selected at the last minute.
- Poor teaching mechanics—use overhead transparencies with tiny print, speak too fast for students to take notes, too much writing on the blackboard, standing in front of the blackboard.
- Poor testing and examination procedures, unfair or confusing grading.
- Negative mannerisms—distracting gestures and facial movements, inappropriate attire.
- Poor speaking skills—monotone voice, speak too fast or too softly, bad grammar, ramble, swear, get sidetracked on irrelevant topics.
- Disrespectful of class time—come in late and stop early.
- Don't want to be interrupted with student questions, talk down to students, sarcasm, act superior.
- Not helpful to students, unapproachable.

Practical Suggestions

What do you do when a teacher is less than ideal? Do you get distressed? Complain? Not study?

By now we hope you have realized that finding a really good match between yourself and an instructor does not happen all the time. As an alternative to feeling like a victim and blaming the instructor for your poor grade, we have the following suggestions:

1. Before registration ask around to find out about various instructors. If you have a choice between instructors, you'll know which one to choose.

2. Try to get as much out of every course as you can, regardless of who your instructor is or how much the teaching style does not fit your preferred learning style. Be open to try a new way of learning.

3. When you have a difficulty understanding what is happening in a course, make an appointment to talk with the instructor. Be prepared to ask for what you want.

4. If you still have problems, go to the office or center that teaches studying and reading skills. The specialists there can be very helpful.

How to Influence Your Instructors

Give Feedback to Instructors

You can influence how your instructors teach. When an instructor does something you appreciate, let them know right away. Don't wait until you fill out the course evaluation at the end of the course. After class, compliment them or hand them a note. When you and the other students praise good teaching, you'll get more of what you like and less of what you don't like.

If you want to tell an instructor that there is something that needs to be improved, give a specific example of what you don't like and what you would like.

How to Turn a Bad Situation Around

So here you are, you totally blew the mid-term, got a D on your project and could end up with a D or F in the course. Is your situation hopeless? Not at all. You can often salvage a bad grade.

Make an appointment to talk with your instructor. *Go with a plan!* If you did poorly on the mid-term or even on the final, ask to take the make-up exam. Ask for a chance to show that you do know the material. Ask if you can write an extra paper or rewrite the project you threw together the night before it was due. Explain why you wish to do better. Instructors are much more inclined to give students a chance when they admit they have done poorly and want to turn things around.

Even if the instructor says you cannot take the test to change your grade, ask to take it anyway to see for yourself if you can do better. Assuming that you will get a better score, this will have a psychological effect on the instructor later.

Most instructors will give you a chance. A bad grade is not inevitable unless you allow it to be. A sincere request for another chance, a specific plan about what you will do, and commitment to do it will influence most instructors.

▐▌▶ WARNING: Do not just walk away from a class where you are doing poorly. Officially drop the class. A failing grade turned in at the end of the course becomes part of your permanent school record.

> One of my early learning experiences involved messing up on a mid-term exam. There was no make-up exam. I felt desperate. I wrote out three questions that could be used as the basis for writing long essays. Then I went to the instructor and asked if I could get extra credit for researching and answering one or more of the three questions. I said I would write my answers in the form of a paper using information from outside the textbook. I was delighted when he agreed to my request. I ended up with a B in the course. The results would have been different if I had not done the extra credit work.—MK

Consider Taking an Incomplete

If you anticipate a bad grade in a course because you have not been able to get all of the work in, and you want to earn a good grade, then consider asking the instructor for an *incomplete*. Usually, you will have to fill out a form and submit it to your instructor before you can receive an incomplete. All colleges have policies for allowing students to complete course work after the course is over. At most colleges you have at least a year.

Courses Can be Repeated

You can change the past if you want to. If you get a low grade in an important subject you can repeat the course to replace a low grade with a higher one. Repeating a course is always an option.

Instructors Are Human!

You will have great instructors, average instructors, and some that you believe are teaching only because they couldn't hold a job out in the real world. The point is that instructors are human beings who vary in their teaching styles and who react just as you do to the way they are treated. You can influence the quality of the teaching you get.

Action Review: Understanding Differences Between Teaching and Learning Styles

❑ When I don't relate to the way an instructor teaches, do I look to see if there is a conflict between my learning style and the instructor's teaching style?

❑ Do I take steps to compensate for my natural preferences, as listed below, in classes with instructors who have different styles?

external direction — internal direction
auditory — visual
extroverted — introverted
left brain (thinking) — right brain (feeling)
sensible — intuitive
judging — perceiving

❑ Have I examined my assumptions about instructors and developed a more realistic and tolerant attitude?

Action Project for Getting Better Teaching

1. Talk with several classmates about what you like best about instructors. Make a list of specific actions you see as desirable.

2. Make a list of ways you could give positive feedback to an instructor when he or she does things you appreciate.
3. Give instructors positive feedback when they do what you want. Let instructors know what you appreciate.

Support Group Activity

Talk about how conflicts between teaching styles and learning styles may be able to explain difficulties you have had with instructors in the past. Work with each other to develop a plan for handling future conflicts.

Discuss how the information in this chapter explains personality conflicts you've had at home or at work. Can you recognize any of your relatives, co-workers or managers in these descriptions?

Talk about some of your past experiences with good instructors and poor instructors. Talk about your teaching experiences as parents or managers. How easy is it? What feedback did you appreciate from people you tried to teach?

Chapter 9

Your Family and Friends: How to Gain Their Support and Encouragement

Do you feel guilty about doing something just for yourself?

Can you ask people for help when you need it?

Do you wonder if you will upset your family or your friends because you are going to school?

Do you know how to develop and follow a positive plan of action for getting the help and support you need?

Do you understand what it means to give high-quality time to others?

There's a Way, If You Will...

Your family and friends do not have to feel deprived by the extra time you spend in school. If mealtime conversation is filled with interesting conversational tidbits, if dreams of an exciting tomorrow are shared with those who are close, and they see a happier, more enthusiastic person, they will be glad for you.

You Can Make It Work

Making the pieces fit, maintaining relationships and school successfully takes time and planning. You will not find all the adjustments or solutions overnight. Fitting into a new role is never easy and it may take six months to a year before you and those close to you have made the transition.

Getting an education is the best insurance you can buy for a successful, secure future. Learning is a lifelong experience. Finding the right combination for relationships, work, and school can pay off big dividends in personal and professional satisfaction.

How to Gain the Support You Need

Here is a simple and effective way to get support, help, encouragement, and understanding from your family and friends:

1. Take some time privately to think about the support you need from others in your new role as a student.

2. Decide to seek that support.

3. Talk to the people whose support you are seeking. Explain why going to school is important to you. Ask what worries they might have and listen with understanding. Ask what positive feelings they have about your going back to school and what advantages they may see for themselves.

4. Be very specific in asking for the support you need— undisturbed time alone, encouragement, household chores done, etc.

5. Track positives with people. Reward any actions you regard as positive, helpful, or supportive with thanks and appreciation. Give others immediate feedback about what you like.

Plan Ahead

Think through what you want to talk about and what requests you will make. Select the best time to talk.

Taking night classes may mean that the family mealtime will be disrupted. If you are working full time and going to school part time, you will have less time together. Find out how they feel about this change and empathize with their concerns rather than telling them not to feel the way they do. Let them know that your time together is important to you.

If people are reluctant to talk about what is ahead, make some effort to get them to think about the months and years ahead. It is essential to keep the lines of communication open to avoid a big blowup someday at just the wrong time.

Don't assume the worst, you may be surprised!

> Before I started to school I sat down with the three teenage children who were still at home and talked with them about what changes might occur in their lives as a result of my commitment to school. The kids were wonderful! They encouraged me so heartily I should have been suspicious, but I wasn't....Years later, after they were out of high school, they told me they were eager to get me involved elsewhere so that they would have more freedom to come and go as they wanted! —MK

Let People Know What You Want

Students with families have requests such as these:

+ I would like my three teenage children to do more housework, so that I will have more time for my studies.
+ I'd like my husband and kids to fix dinner for themselves a couple of nights a week when I am at class.

◆ It would be nice to have my wife ask me about my courses and spend a little time talking about my experiences as a student.

◆ I'd appreciate being left alone to study three nights a week; that means not knocking on my door or interrupting to tell me about something on TV.

Why don't people get what they want? The answer is surprising. They usually have not asked.

Most of us were raised not to be selfish. Some selfishness is essential, however, when expressed in a way that is not demanding.

Most people report that once they have the courage to ask for support, they receive far more than they expected. Some students report that when they finally ask for what they want, the reply is "Why didn't you ask before? Sure, I'll be glad to do that!"

Getting Help at Home

Anyone who manages a home knows there are certain mainte-nance tasks that must be done—homework, or not. When dirty socks and underwear carpet the floor, it is time for some coop-eration and delegation. Most children over the age of seven, and most partners, can learn to pick up, sort, and put the clothes in the washing machine.

Even a four-year-old can help fold clothes and put them away. To reverse an old quote, "Ask not what you can do for others, but what can they do for you!" As roles change, it is time to delegate responsibilities to other household members.

Have a meeting with the family each week to develop a chore schedule. On a piece of paper, list the jobs each person agrees to do and specify when it will be done. It helps to rotate the responsibility for developing the weekly list to others. Par-ticipate in the discussion, of course, but when you have some-one else write down the various duties and place the list in a conspicuous place, it will seem less imposed by you.

Post your own weekly time schedule in a conspicuous place so that all can see where you will be and when. When members of your household see that Thursday evening from 7:30 to 9:00 is a study period, they will be more likely to leave you alone, *especially if you stick with your own schedule!*

▐▌▌▶ TIP: Others will be less likely to interrupt or intrude during your study hours if you set aside specific times during the week for each important person.

Quality is Better Than Quantity

Reserve one solid hour each week for each important person. Others will be less demanding when they know they have their own special time with you. For example, talk with your daughter Cheryl about when she'd like her hour. Write "Cheryl's hour" in big letters on your schedule. Then make sure she gets her hour with you. Do not try to fit more than one person into the same hour. Make these hours very important to you. Avoid missing one or changing one if you possibly can.

Let the others decide what will be done during their hour. Self-esteem develops or is maintained by being in close contact with others, by being seen as unique, by feeling important, and from being able to influence the world. So don't plan this hour, let the person influence what you do together.

Be curious about what develops. Many people who have done this report that their personal relationships and contacts with family members improve significantly.

Working together on tasks at home can be important time together. As one sets the table, another scrubs the potatoes, someone unloads the dishwasher, and the microwave zaps the main course, each person talks about their day. Time for sharing is essential when you have to juggle work, home, and school. Sharing, caring, and doing the work together can all be done at the same time.

Use a Little Psychology

Thousands of experiments conducted by psychologists over the years have established the validity of a principle that affects the actions of others. The principle is:

⟶ *Actions that are rewarded tend to increase.*

Consequently,

1. If you thank, compliment, and reward others for doing what is helpful to you they will do even more.
2. If you stop rewarding, they'll do less of what is helpful.

What rewards can you use? Here is a list of suggestions from adult students about things they've done:

◆ Express appreciation.
◆ Say "thank you."
◆ Buy or fix their favorite food for them.
◆ Give hugs and kisses.
◆ Give treats or little gifts.
◆ Be interested in their lives.
◆ Tell them about something interesting at school.
◆ Speak highly of them to others.
◆ Give them back rubs and neck massages.
◆ Let them feel that your success is their success.
◆ Ask what they would like from you.
◆ Leave nice notes for them; send cards.

When you speak clearly about what you would like from others and then follow up with "thank-you's" and rewards, you usually get results that exceed your expectations. Most people respond in very positive ways. In fact, you may be over-whelmed by all the love and support others show you.

Expect Surprises

Expect some surprises and be prepared to make some adjust-ments of your own when your life changes. Letting people do things their own way may be difficult at first, but a positive attitude and a sense of humor can pull you through.

In one family, for example, the children (grade-school age) volunteered to cook dinner one evening a week. They accepted full responsibility for shopping, cooking, and cleaning up afterward. Their mother said she assumed the meal would be done the way she always did it. She reported:

> The first time they "cooked" dinner they met me at the door all excited and led me to the dining room before I could take off my coat. I expected steaming plates with vegetables, salad, and so forth. When I walked in my eyes almost fell out of my head. Their idea of a great dinner was boiled hot dogs served on paper plates with a bottle of pop, a bag of potato chips, and Twinkies for dessert! I didn't know whether to collapse in hysterical laughter or lecture them on the right way to shop, cook, and serve a nutritious meal. I did neither. As I sat there eating a barely warm wiener, I told myself it wouldn't kill me to let them do it their way. I've had some interesting meals since then. Peanut butter sandwiches and pie aren't too bad. And the paper plates are real time and energy savers.

Things Don't Always Work Out

Some students find that their home situations do not get better. Some family members may become difficult. A partner may start to drink more or stay out late. Children may begin to get into trouble or have difficulty at school.

If anything this extreme takes place, it is important to seek professional advice and counseling. Get to know what services are available at the college. There are many experts you can talk to and a variety of sources of help. Other students can provide support and practical advice. Ask around and you are likely to discover that more good solutions are possible than you imagined.

They Need Emotional Support
It can be easy to forget that family and friends need some nurturing, too. An instructor once said to an over-achieving beginner, "When it comes to a choice of studying extra to get an A on the mid-term, working overtime, or taking your children

to the zoo—take the kids to the zoo." A little attention in time saves resentment in the long run.

When you return to school, people close to you may react as though you are changing the rules on them. A change in your daily routines forces them to change theirs, and they may resist.

Adult students find the return easier if they are prepared for the mixed emotions that others may have about their changed roles. It helps to understand their feelings, and then help them see that your going back to school is good for them as well.

Bev had four children when she decided to return to school. Two seemed to adjust fine to the new schedule, but one daughter was getting more "mouthy" and her son said resentfully, "Why can't you be like other mommies and just stay home?"

The next term Bev scheduled classes so she could be at home when the children came home from school. She started a ten-minute contact time for each child where sharing the day and hugging and touching was made a priority when they first came home. The discipline and resentment problems disappeared.

It May Take a While

The more your family and friends have been dependent on you, the more difficult it will be for them to be more responsible for themselves. If you meet resistance, the change can be difficult. They may become upset and refuse to talk. They may accuse you of being selfish and of not caring about them.

There are many reasons for such reactions. A husband may secretly fear that if his wife becomes capable, educated, and employable, she may decide to leave. A wife may feel neglected having her husband work full time and then devote evenings and weekends to school. Your friends miss your calls.

Try to not let others make you feel guilty if they become upset. Let them know you understand their feelings but don't take too much responsibility for their unhappy reactions. Would you let a ten-year-old control how you drive or where you go? Are others better qualified to make decisions about your life than you are? Does your partner know your needs better than you do?

Hold true to your plan for yourself while you give others time to adjust to this new way of life. Let them know how important they are to you.

Develop a Plan and Be Positive

Going to school can solve problems. Try to use your returning to school as an opportunity to improve your relationship with your loved ones. Healthful relationships are based on people's supporting each other's growth and development, not dependence. Your returning to school could lead to deeper, closer, and warmer feelings of love and appreciation than you ever thought possible.

George was feeling out of touch with his wife, Kathy. They both worked and went to school. It seemed they never talked anymore.

Together they looked at both of their schedules. They made Wednesday lunch and Sunday morning brunch dates top priorities. George says now: "I'd never think of missing one of these dates. That is the time we still know we are in tune with each other and share our triumphs and frustrations. We are back to being best friends."

Include Them

Make them feel included in your world, not excluded. Try to create the feeling "We are going to college." If your instructor will allow a visit, and if appropriate, consider taking a family member or friend to a class.

The more they know about what you do, the more they can understand and support you. A Saturday tour around campus can help introduce them to your new world. Take your spouse or older children to athletic events or concerts. Find out if they can use the Physical Education facilities. Bring them to the library with you some evening.

Going back to school can be the best gift you give school-age children. As they study, you study. The message comes through loud and clear; education is a priority here. Gathering together to do your homework can be much more bonding than "zoning out" in front of the TV.

Also, when children know you struggle with school, it gets you off the parental pedestal and on a level leading to better understanding. If your child can help you learn math, so much the better. If they can help demystify the world of computers, you both benefit!

Family and friends need to know they are still a priority in your life. Give them good quality time. Time will be treasured more as the demands of school increase. TV and for fun reading may bite the dust, but good personal relationships are an essential success foundation as you juggle work, home, and school.

Action Review: Checklist of Useful Actions

❑ Have I talked with others about returning to school and how this will affect our lives?

❑ Have I listened well to the concerns of others?

❑ Have I asked for support in a direct, clear, and specific way?

❑ Can I ask for what I need without feeling guilty or demanding?

❑ Do I tell people often enough how much I appreciate their efforts to help?

❑ Do I have a variety of reinforcements available that I can use to express appreciation?

❑ Have I acquainted myself with all the professional resources available to me at school in case I need advice?

❑ Do I have an active, positive plan to make things work out?

Support Group Activity

Talk with each other about what you have done to enlist the support of others. Discuss how it feels to make selfish requests. Help each other find ways to handle challenges. Compliment each other for progress you have made. Be sure to tell each other about amusing incidents and your successes.

Chapter 10

How to Balance Going to College with Working

Do you know over 50% of all adult college students work part or full time?

Do you know part-time college students account for the greatest increase in college population?

Do you know most careers will require you to be a life-long learner?

Do you know you can earn college credit by combining work and school?

Scheduling Work and School

Colleges and employers have responded to the needs of students who work. The times and places you take your college classes are becoming more flexible. Evening and weekend courses are available. Distance Learning and online classes are increasing in popularity.

If your working hours are flexible you may be able to schedule your courses on Mondays, Wednesdays, and Fridays only, or just mornings or afternoons to accommodate your job. Some companies will arrange a four day work week so you can take three day seminars or attend weekend classes.

Note also that *you do not have to take all of your courses from the same college!* If a course at another nearby college fits your schedule better or offers courses you need online, you may be able to take that course and transfer the credit. Transferring credit is easy to do between state-supported colleges. Be sure to find out if the colleges are using the same quarter or semester school year system. Quarter length courses do not qualify for semester length credit.

Course-Load Guidelines

If you work full time, you probably should take no more than two classes in college at one time. The rule of thumb: for every hour of class time, you need two or three hours to do the homework for that class. Thus, if you spend six hours a week in class, you will spend 12 to 18 hours a week in preparation. Add that to a 40-hour work week and you have a sizable commitment. Travel time from work, home and school must also be considered.

If you are going to school full time, work outside school should be kept to 20 or fewer hours. If you work more than 20 hours, work, school, or both are likely to suffer from the overload.

A few students choose jobs that pay less if studying is possible at times on the job. Some students know they need the physical release of a lot of activity after classes and deliberately choose a job involving physical labor.

Work-study jobs can allow split-shift work around class schedules. For some, splitting up school and work is helpful; for others, it is fragmenting. There is no right or wrong way to combine work and school, but there is a way that works best for you. The challenge is to find it.

Employers Will Help You

Employers need educated workers. They need people who learn new technology rapidly, work well as a team member, communicate effectively in words and writing, and adapt to a rapidly changing work world.

In recent years employers have created many ways to encourage, support, and pay for the education of the workers they need. It is estimated that industry now spends from $40 to $60 billion on educational training each year. Employers work closely with colleges to offer a variety of ways to blend working with your college education.

Merging Learning and Work

Most colleges now offer programs for getting college credit for work experience. Credit is offered in a variety of ways that include cooperative education, work-study programs, internships, and practicums.

Cooperative Work Experience
Cooperative work experience allows a student to work and earn college credit while exploring a career choice. When a student has chosen a major such as business, computer science, or engineering, the school's cooperative education department can help arrange work experience in the field.

A student may have a particular job site in mind, or the cooperative work specialist may find an appropriate work placement in the student's major field of study. Specific learning experiences are defined and the student is supervised in meeting the objectives. The average co-op student earns $7,000 per year, although some placements are arranged on a volunteer basis.

Cooperative education personnel maintain close contact with companies designated as co-op sites. Everything is done to ensure a good learning experience.

It is not possible to receive retroactive credit in co-op, but it is possible to earn college credit for present employment. If your present work is within the field of your college major, or you are doing certain kinds of work to see if you wish to make it your major field of study, it is worth contacting your cooperative education department to look into the possibility of receiving college credit for your present job.

Work Study and Student Help

Colleges hire many students to work on campus. The federal government provides funds for the college work-study program. Work-study students must qualify for their jobs by showing financial need.

Student-help jobs are also available. They require only that the student is competent to do the work.

Those in the work-study and student-help programs fill in at libraries, locker rooms, receptionists' desks, laboratories, cafeterias, counseling offices, school grounds, and many other college locations. Usually, they work for the minimum wage but the work experience can be valuable training. It can help clarify career goals and be included on a résumé. These jobs often allow you some study time on the job and your supervisor shifts your work hours to fit your class schedule and exam times.

Everyone Benefits

If you haven't had much paid work experience, a work-study job can be a good confidence builder. It is a way to prove your worth in the work world. The recent trend is for more organizations to offer positions to students. They recognize that involving students in work experience is a good way to screen potential employees. It also helps the work-study student to build job contacts.

Joan, for example, was a single parent struggling to get off welfare. She started working for the counseling department in a clerical capacity as a work-study student. Her work and life experience helped solidify her choice of social work as a college major. The department was able to set up a co-op work experience to help her earn college credits. Later, when Joan needed a practicum site for her degree, the counseling department set up an information referral position in job placement. When she was granted her degree in social work, Joan had incorporated enough practical, professional experience to have a decided edge on other graduates. Valuable contacts and recommendations were hers. Securing a job, using her new credentials, was not difficult.

Internship Programs
An internship is a training position that usually pays you for acquiring a skill. Internships may be offered where expensive equipment or the need for highly trained professionals make on-the-job training cost effective. Prerequisite skills are taught in the classroom, but most of the new learning takes place in the work place.

Two vocational career fields that use internships extensively are electronic engineering technician and radio/TV broadcasting. These industries grow and change so rapidly that few colleges have the funds or facilities for the latest equipment. Neither can the colleges meet salary scales to hire top people in these fields.

A partnership is formed where education experts break the learning process into manageable steps, write the curriculum, assign credit, provide on-site consultation, and see that complementary classwork is provided. Internship programs often lead to a two-year associate degree, or may be a requirement for an advanced degree.

Practicum Training Experiences
Practicum experiences differ from internships in that they often require a year or more of classroom work before a student is allowed on-the-job practical experience. Paraprofessional programs (teacher assistant, legal assistant, alcohol/drug counselor) have significant practical experience as an essential part of their vocational degree program.

On-the-job training may take anywhere from three months to more than a year. This practicum training is coupled with classroom discussion and job supervision. (Note: students *rarely* receive payment for practicum experience. The personal supervision you receive from experts is valuable compensation.)

Balancing Predictable School and Work Demands

Many jobs have peak demand periods. In school, it's mid-terms and finals. In retail sales, pre-Christmas shopping will keep you hopping. For colleges, fall registration is a busy time for support services. If you have school-age children summer vacation can be extra demanding.

When work times are predictably busy, lighten your school load to accommodate busy times. Get that paper in early; move ahead in your reading; talk with your teacher to get a jump on early work—or an approved delay, if needed.

For those who juggle work and school, knowing about and using your options are survival tools. Trying to cram full-time work, full-time school, and demanding personal relationships into twenty-four hours can lead a person to early burnout. It is not how fast you can get there, but rather, are you enjoying the process? Can you go the distance? That's what counts!

Basic Income Jobs (that don't interfere with academic success)

If you need to work while you go to school, don't expect to have your dream job. You can, however, make it work with your school schedule. It would be a bonus if it were somehow related to your career choice, but it does not have to be connected. What is essential is that you can earn a certain amount of money to take care of basic survival.

How do you find such a job? The same rules apply here that you use searching for career employment.

~ For more information on finding a Basic Income Job, see our web site: http://www.adultstudent.com/

College, Work, Family, Friends, and Time For You

The guidelines and suggestions in chapters 9 and 10 are being used successfully by many students. It is possible to combine going to college with studying, family life, a job, and still have time for yourself too. Here is what one student reported:

> I had no idea how many hours of studying were necessary for class. I found myself adding up the hours in a week and realized something would have to give. I sat down and developed my "Study Schedule," my "Me-Time Schedule," my "Family Schedule," and finally, my "Work Schedule." Now my time is allocated so that I can make the best use of it.

Many students find that when they organize their time better, ask others for help or understanding, and work only on the most important things to be done, they can accomplish much more than they ever thought possible. As we've said before, you don't have to be an extraordinary person to succeed in college. All you have to do is be in control of what you do with yourself.

Action Review

Check the following list for balancing work and school:

❏ Do I make realistic school and work demands on myself?

❏ Have I explored the possibility of getting college credit for work experience?

❏ Have I asked my employer about ways that my educational efforts could be paid for or reimbursed?

❏ Have I looked at new developments and changes in the job market?

❏ Have I combined employment with career development opportunities?

Support Group Activity

Do the members of your group work? What sort of balance between work and study have you each arranged? What do you know about ways to work for pay, earn college credit, and gain on-the-job experience? Does someone in your group have some job information you can use?

Chapter 11

Celebrating Diversity

Are you aware some of your best education is getting to know and appreciate people from other cultures?

Do you realize that a person's cultural background starts imprinting in earliest childhood?

Are you aware there are more women in college today than men?

Do you know the work world is giving added importance to employees knowing more than one language?

The College Environment Is Like the Work World

Today's workplace requires skills at understanding and working with people from different ethnic and cultural backgrounds. The dynamics involved in personal interactions in college are similar to those found in the work world.

College is not just a place to get new information. It is a place where exchanging views, learning about different life styles, getting new perspectives, and gaining insights can open up paths that lead to a more satisfying life. The college setting is a safe place where the pay check is not threatened when you discuss, argue, exchange views, adapt to other's differences, try new things, and meet new people. This is why some of your most important learning in college is of an interpersonal nature, not just an academic one.

Demographics and Attitudes Are Changing

The United States has been known as a "melting pot" for different cultures and ethnic groups. An attitude that existed among many was, "Learn our language, customs, and values. If you can not fit in here, go somewhere else."

We are a very young country, and maybe could be excused for some of our tunnel vision in the past. Social awareness and current events, however, show that "melting pot" idealism has not worked very well. Social unrest along with a rapid increase in minority populations has shifted attitudes toward the necessity of respecting and understanding differences in people's languages, cultural heritage, family roots, customs, and values.

Native Americans lived in this land for thousands of years, respecting the trees, waters, land and sky. They did not believe in individual ownership of these resources, but believed they belonged to all. Their respect for nature, often dismissed by whites, is now known to be critical to the survival of our environment. Preserving the resources of this earth are now seen as an essential value by many.

African Americans were brought to this country with the shackles of slavery curbing their freedom. They bonded together forming strong ties to family and churches to gain comfort and find ways to survive in a hostile society. The strength of these ties is now recognized and seen as a model for others to copy.

People of Hispanic background come in ever increasing numbers to the United States, hoping for a better life. The richness of their language and culture is serving as incentive for many people to become bilingual.

Asian immigrants bring a wealth of languages and a strong work ethic to this country. To build a future for their families they often combine full time school and full time work. This reminds us of the hard work and pioneering spirit that built this country.

Older students, with the variety of work and life experience, bring the perspective of generations to understanding current events as well as course content.

The Gift of a Broader View

Prejudice handicaps learning. People from different backgrounds, religions, and cultures provide a perspective to life, work and education that allows a richer learning environment. To ignore this source of added value to your education would be to deprive yourself of one of your greatest opportunities. There are many academic, social, political, and career decisions ahead of you. Developing empathy and understanding for the views, values, and visions of others is a survival skill as well as a gift of personal enrichment.

Changing Faces in Our Cities

In American cities the population mix is shifting rapidly. At present, in New York City about 20% of the population is African American, 20% are foreign born. In Dallas-Fort Worth about 15% are African American, 20% foreign born, and 15% are Hispanic. In San Francisco-Oakland-San Jose about 10% are African American, 20% are foreign born, and 18% are Hispanic. The Hispanic population is our fastest growing minority group. According to projections, in a few decades white Euro-Americans will be less than 50% of the U.S. population.

College Campuses Reflect the Cultural Shift

On college campuses white Euro-Americans now make up less than 80% of the college population. At the University of California at Berkeley, white Euro-Americans are less than 50% of the students enrolled.

Almost 55% of the students in college are women. The traditionally male universities such as Harvard, Yale, and Princeton are now seeking a gender balance and are actively recruiting women students. The same is true of women's colleges as many of them recruit men to their campuses. One result of this is that the male dominated professions such as law, engineering, and medicine are seeing great increases in women students.

Students who are over twenty-five, are seen in greater numbers at campuses all over the United States. Smaller families, decreased family obligations, changing work world, financial pressure and/or ability, and intellectual curiosity all contribute to this changing scene.

We each come to college with cultural, social, economic, and political backgrounds that we started absorbing in our early childhood. What games did we play? Were we raised in a small family or in a large family with friends and relatives also important in our upbringing?

Was education looked on as an important value? Which was more important, taking care of your self or taking care of your family? How do your present ideas and values differ from the family you were raised in? If some values differ, was the changing easy or difficult?

Were you encouraged to learn a second language by your family? Discouraged from doing so?

> ⫸ In the years ahead being bilingual will greatly increase your chances for employment and career success.

The Price May Be High But the Benefit is Bigger

Comparing your personal history to others, whether in the family, your neighborhood, your work, or at school can be challenging, frustrating, and rewarding. Differences in the way things are viewed and handled can lead to conflict. Change does not come about easily. On a personal level, you have to decide how much you wish to increase your tolerance and comfort level with people much different than you.

A major barrier to decreasing prejudice is found in the attitudes of close friends and family. If you made friends with someone from a different race or background, how would your friends and family react if they found out? Are your friendships determined by what is acceptable to others? It can be a dilemma.

Keep in mind also that learning to fit into society so that you can be successful does not mean giving up your culture or values. Indian students, for example, find that going to pow wows and maintaining connections with their elders and spiritual leaders gives them strength and stability that many white students lack. Finding the right balance for you is a "do-it-yourself" job.

If your background or present situation makes you feel different and conflict and confusion arises, it can be helpful to talk about the struggle with family members, friends, and counselors. The struggle can be great but the rewards can be greater. It will prepare you for the world of tomorrow in which you will become an active participant in making a better life for yourself and others.

Different Backgrounds Can Create Difficulties

Your culture may tell you to listen quietly and respectfully to those in authority and not to question their views. Yet, the professor urges you to participate by asking questions and challenging his ideas.

You may have been raised to think that as a female you are not to meet a male's eyes. Yet, the instructor interprets the lack of eye contact as a sign of disinterest.

Your sense of time may be more in tune with showing an appreciation of seasonal changes than with the discipline of studying the week before finals. This could bring you a lower grade in a class weighted heavily toward tests.

You may have been raised to be very verbal and express your feelings with passion, but now you receive negative comments for your long emotional statements in class.

Your instructor is impressed with your skill in math and science and encourages you to make engineering your major, but being female you know your family will only encourage your brothers to earn professional degrees. You are to be a clerical worker.

Your instructor comes highly recommended for her knowledge in your field of study, but you can not understand her because of a heavy accent.

These are all examples of how culture background, yours or someone else's, plays a role in your decisions as a student. These cultural differences also affect your personal relations.

On The Homefront, Roles Are Re-examined

If no one in your family has ever gone to college before, your family may not understand the many hours of study you must do when you get home. They think you are drawing away from them and have become less important to you. You see time spent studying as the best way to help your family.

You have always been interested in how things work and the idea of studying auto mechanics appeals to you but your family says you will study international business. American students seem to make choices just for themselves, not for the good of their families. Should individual choice be more important than family choice? Values are different here. Change brings conflict yet affords the opportunity to grow and reexamine.

Personal Touch versus Institutional Distance

If you like to have lots of friends, like to know many people by name and have many others knowing you by name, the apparent coldness of a large institution with many rules and regulations can feel very uncomfortable. You may feel like a walking social security number, rather than your real self.

Has your background emphasized formal manners, where

the hierarchy of authority is clearly defined and respected? If so, it may be hard to relate to the casual, informal, egalitarian approach of American students who insist on their personal rights regardless of group needs.

The straight lecture method where the student takes notes may be what you are used to. If so, you may now feel confused by the discussion, interaction, and questioning that is expected of you in some of your classes. All of this requires adjustment on your part and may test your patience.

Many Advantages

Instead of retaining a view of the U.S. as a "melting pot," the image of a "stir fry" may be more appropriate. In a stir fry each ingredient is separate, but adds to the flavor and distinction of the entire dish. It is time to breath new life into our personal and national recipe, to change the metaphor to allow a more international flavor.

Class discussions, support groups, campus social activities, student government, meal times in the cafeteria, and the college newspaper all afford opportunity for exchanging social, philosophical, political, and personal views. Students from different ethnic and cultural backgrounds have special conferences and celebrations open for everyone to attend.

It is in this way we can gain the intellectual and personal insights which allow us to take an educated and humane place in our world culture. We are all teachers and we are all learners!

Action Review

☐ Have I examined how cultural influences affect my reactions to others and the choices I make?

☐ Am I aware of how different cultural views affect people's work and life styles?

☐ Do I see the benefits to be gained from increased awareness of other cultures?

❑ Have I made efforts to know, appreciate, and respect people from other cultures?

❑ Have I attended meetings or gatherings put on by students from other cultures at my college?

Support Group Activity

Have each person in your group prepare a personal cultural profile. Include social, political, economic, and religious attitudes in your family of origin. Set up a time when you have lunch with at least two students of significantly different backgrounds. Discuss differences and similarities in your cultural profiles. With your study group examine what you learned that was new. What surprised you? What did you have in common?

Are any of you bilingual? Talk about how being bilingual would affect your lives.

Chapter 12

How to Handle
Pressure Well

Do you know the difference between stress and strain?

Do you believe the way for your life to get better is for other people to change?

Did you know stress can be good for you?

Can you be both optimistic and pessimistic?

Do you know how to decrease your negative experiences and increase your positive experiences?

How to Handle Pressure and Strain

Some people deal with pressure better than others. You probably have several friends or acquaintances who are very durable and resilient. They cope well with life's difficulties. You probably also know several people who can turn an ordinary day into a tragedy.

This chapter will show how to hold up well under the many pressures that can build up when you have to attend classes and study while you handle other important responsibilities, work, and raise a family. Before we look at practical ways to increase your resiliency, however, we need to clarify some misunderstandings about stress.

Stress has received a bad name in recent years. Many people think stress is bad. It isn't. *Too much* stress may be bad for you, but a certain amount is necessary for health and well-being.

Dr. Selye made a mistake.
Much of the misunderstanding about stress traces back to Dr. Hans Selye, the physician who created the concept *biological stress* in 1936. After decades of writing and speaking about stress, however, he apologized in his memoirs for using the wrong term. He explained that when he came from Europe to attend medical school he did not understand either the English language or physics very well. He said his research was about strain, not stress. He said he should have named his concept the *strain syndrome.*

There is no "stress" in any situation until a person experiences strain they don't like.
In physics a stressor is an external force attempting to deform an object. The effect on an object is measured as strain. What is a mild strain for one person is extreme stress for another person in the same situation.

Many people blame the situation for their reaction to it.
It is not unusual to hear people claim that they have stressful jobs, stresses at home, or stresses as college students. That is a

misperception. They are confusing the situation with their reaction to it. It isn't the circumstance itself, it is your reaction to it that counts. What is distressing for one person is an easy workout for another. An instructor that one student complains about for being extremely tough is appreciated by another for setting high standards.

Stressful situations can be beneficial.
Dr. Selye coined the term *eustress* to emphasize that everyone needs a certain level of stress. When we work at handling the strains we engage, we gradually get stronger. Athletes build up their physical strength with frequent workouts. Professional training programs build competence by straining people to their limits. Emotionally stressful experiences can motivate people to learn new coping skills. Some mothers, for example, handle the addition of a fourth child to the family more easily than they handled having their first child.

Stress Resistant Personalities

Two people in an identical situation will have different reactions to it. Some mothers enjoy talking about their amusing experiences raising a family. Other mothers are so distressed trying to raise their families they need tranquilizers, counseling, and emotional support.

The situation a person is in is not the problem. *It is how a person deals with a situation* that explains why some people become sick while others become strong in the same environment. The following list summarizes the research findings about persons less likely to develop stress related illness. As you read the list check to see how well it describes you:

___ few upsetting events in routine activities;

___ feel capable of taking effective action about upsetting events;

___ draw action choices from a wide range of inner and external resources;

___ experience family and friends as caring and supportive;

___ manage self-change well; and

___ convert negative experiences into beneficial learning.

Recognize the Signs of Not Coping Well

Indicators that the pressures are getting to be too much include: sleepless nights, drinking alcohol to get to sleep, losing your temper over a minor incident, migraine headaches, frequent colds and illnesses, auto accidents, ulcers flaring up, high blood pressure and other cardiovascular problems, losing track of time, falling asleep in class, and forgetting to bring a paper you stayed up late at night to finish.

How to Cope Effectively With Lots of Pressures

For most adult students, the challenge is not having to deal with one major difficulty, the challenge is how to hold up week after week handling a whole lot of little things.

It is important to avoid feeling helpless and at the mercy of external forces. Here is a practical plan of action for decreasing emotional strain while increasing your hardiness and resiliency.

Decrease the pressures.

1. *Make a list of everything you experience as negative, upsetting, or stressful.*

   Sometimes the only way to be more positive is let yourself be negative. When you make a list of everything you feel pressured about, you are not a negative person, you are an emotionally healthy person taking the first step toward coping well. Listing all the forces working against you is the first step for preparing to deal with them.

2. *Express your feelings about your list.*

   It is not unusual to experience some physical and emotional upsets when you start college for the first time. Forgetfulness, stomach and intestinal problems, and sleeping difficulties are normal reactions to stress. These symptoms are usually temporary and should diminish quickly if you find outlets for your feelings.

3. *Go through your list, item by item, asking questions:*

- ✦ Could I do something about this? How direct is my contact?
- ✦ What if I ignored this or avoided contact?
- ✦ Could I change the situation in some way? Who could help me?
- ✦ What if I changed my reaction to it?

The aim is to find ways to minimize the impact of the entire list. It isn't usually one big thing that does a person in, it is the accumulation of many little things. With this plan you diminish the effects of too many strains, avoid feeling helpless, and increase feelings of control.

> Although I'm a pretty relaxed person most of the time, I did learn to recognize when stress was building up. I finally figured out that from time to time I would develop this overwhelming urge to clean the house, which meant that I was feeling too much pressure. I knew that things were really bad when the urge to clean the house changed and became specific—*I wanted to clean the refrigerator!*—MK

Increase positive and revitalizing experiences.

1. *Make a list of things you experience as positive in your life.*
   Ask yourself what activities make you feel happy and relaxed. What makes you feel good? Reflect on pleasant experiences.

2. *Ask questions about how to repeat, increase, or have new positive experiences.*

- ✦Am I ignoring or taking for granted some positive aspects?
- ✦What do I enjoy doing? What do I get enthusiastic about?
- ✦What would I like to do that I keep putting off?
- ✦With whom do I enjoy sharing good experiences?

3. *Do several things good for you to do.*

It is important to be self-nourishing even though it may look like selfishness. Psychologically healthy people are both unselfish and selfish. They act in ways that are good for their well-being while still being helpful to others.

Develop Healthy Self-Esteem

Your self-esteem influences how well you do in college and in life. Many people were trained by their parents to never brag, be stuck up, or conceited. As a result, many people have never developed a healthy level of self-esteem. It takes courage to defy old parental prohibitions, but it must be done to achieve and enjoy success.

Without strong self-esteem you will probably find it difficult to even imagine getting a high grade point average. Your expectations and actions are controlled by worries about what others might think. You are afraid that if you got top grades others would think that you think you are superior to them.

Self-esteem is your opinion of yourself. Strong self-esteem is like a thick emotional skin. It acts as a buffer to shrug off hurtful criticisms. When someone is critical, your self-esteem lets you decide that you like your opinion of yourself better than theirs. Self-esteem lets you appreciate compliments. It determines how much you learn after something goes wrong.

Self-esteem is strengthened by positive self-talk. Make a list of all the things you like and appreciate about yourself.

Overcoming the "Good Child" Handicap

The plan outlined here will decrease feelings of pressure, increase revitalizing experiences, and increase your ability to do well in your courses. It is a simple, effective plan that will increase your hardiness and resiliency.

If you were raised to be a "good girl" or a "good boy" this coping plan will be difficult. You were raised to never be negative, never act in selfish ways, and never be prideful or stuck-up. Your parents had good intentions, but trying to go through life acting like a good five year old is a handicap in a constantly changing world.

Mentally healthy people can list what they are unhappy about, can make requests of others, and include themselves on their list of people they do nice things for. Here are some things to consider doing for yourself:

Revitalizing Activities

Laugh and Play With Friends

Successful students do not study all the time. Do anything you can to prevent your college life from getting too serious, too burdensome, and too heavy. Make a conscious effort to get into activities where you can laugh or play hard and completely forget your responsibilities at school and home.

Stay Physically Active

Do anything each week that works your muscles. This might be bike riding, gardening, jogging, playing racquetball or tennis, swimming, or fast walking. It may be a yoga class. In any case, activities that work your muscles increase your physical tiredness and help you sleep and rest better. If you are not doing much of this now, take another look at the recreation facilities on campus.

Take Naps, Meditate, or Listen to Music

Naps are a wonderful way to relax and revitalize yourself. If you have a car at school, try taking naps in your car. Take a short nap early in the evening instead of watching television before studying. Take naps on weekends if you wish.

Research into meditation shows that it has many beneficial effects. Find a place where you can sit and do nothing for a few minutes each day. Don't use the time to solve problems. Focus your attention on a beautiful scene. Recall one of your most enjoyable vacations. Take easy, relaxing breaths. Most counseling centers have useful books and cassette tapes on how to increase relaxation and reduce stress.

An option is to sit and listen to classical music while

doing nothing else. Sit back and totally lose yourself in the music. The word "music" means something that enhances musing. So do it. Muse.

Becoming Stronger and More Hardy

✦ The ability to handle sustained pressure over a long period of time can be learned. An effective plan of action includes reducing negative, distressing experiences while increasing positive, revitalizing experiences.

✦ By seeing that a stressful experience is an experience of strain that you don't like, you avoid feeling victimized. You can use strain like a workout. Just as bike riding, jogging, or swimming leads to getting physically stronger, using emotional strains as workouts leads to becoming mentally and emotionally stronger.

✦ Remember, it isn't the situation that matters, it is your reaction to it that counts. Martha Washington once observed:
    I am still determined to be cheerful and happy in whatever situation I may be, for I have also learned from experience that the greater part of our happiness or misery depends upon our dispositions and not upon our circumstances.

✦ What is distressing for one person is not stressful for another. When you take steps to cope with pressures and negative experiences, you will experience less stress and strain.

Action Review

❏ I have listed all the things I experience as negative, and developed plans for reducing, changing, avoiding, or minimizing them.

❏ I have listed what is positive and revitalizing for me and have a plan for increasing my pleasant, revitalizing experiences.

❏ I am able to consciously like and appreciate myself.

☐ I understand the feeling of distress is emotional strain and that strain can lead to getting stronger and better.

Support Group Activity

Talk about the pressures you each feel. Ask each other "How do you manage?" Find out what you each do that is enjoyable, positive, and revitalizing.

Discuss your reactions to reading that an important step toward thriving under pressure is to list everything you feel negative about. Was it difficult to express negative feelings?

Talk about how you might have been raised to be a "good child" who never complains, is not selfish, and has low self-esteem.

Discuss how easy or difficult it is to engage in activities that may seem selfish. How have others reacted when you've acted in selfish ways? Discuss your feelings about developing strong self-esteem.

Did a disruptive change such as job loss or divorce lead to your enrolling in college? If so, how well have you dealt with your feelings about this matter?

Chapter 13

Resiliency in a World of Non-Stop Change

Do you understand how curiosity, playfulness, intuition, and humor are related to resiliency?

Do you know how to learn useful lessons from everyday experiences?

Do you know it is healthy to be paradoxical?

Do you know the value of developing an attitude of professionalism?

Resiliency Makes the Difference

Diana Spatz was a single mother on welfare. She encountered many barriers when she tried to get an education to become self-sufficient, but she found ways to overcome the barriers and graduated from college with honors. She now works to help other parents on welfare gain access to funding that is available for their education.

Paul Weiand was a bank executive expecting a big promotion, but he was fired instead. He felt devastated and depressed. Months of self-examination led him to decide to enroll in graduate school. He earned a Ph.D. in psychology, and is founder of the Center for Advanced Emotional Intelligence.

Jackie Leno Grant felt out of place as a Native American in a nearly all-white school in rural Oregon. When she skipped school, the administrators transferred her to reform school. Her unfair treatment could have made her bitter and rebellious, but Jackie studied hard and never got into trouble. She graduated with good grades, got a job and enrolled in a community college. She earned a college degree and became a college advisor working with minority students.

What is Your Response to Adversity?

How do you react to life's difficulties? Do you react like a victim or do you react by coping and learning from the difficulty?

The victim reaction is to be crushed by the blow. The victim habit is to complain: "This isn't fair!" "They've ruined my life." "Look what they've done to me." And "I won't be able to find another job." People with victim patterns feel helpless. They blame others for their unhappy circumstances.

Highly resilient people react to adversity by learning and coping. When hurt and distressed they expect to find a way to have things turn out well.

Resiliency is defined as "the ability to recover quickly from disruptive change, illness, or misfortune without being overwhelmed or acting in dysfunctional ways."

Resilient people are agile, flexible, adapt quickly, changeproficient, learn from experience, gain strength from adversity, and have a talent for serendipity. They handle major difficulties better than most people. When hit by major setbacks they don't complain about life being unfair.

Suzy Kellett, for example, gave birth to quadruplets when she was 31 years old. Her husband couldn't deal with four new born babies and walked out. He left her in their Idaho home to cope with the four infants by herself, with no help and no income to pay the rent and other bills.

Suzy telephoned her parents in Illinois. They volunteered to take them all into their home, so she packed up their few belongings and flew to Chicago—with nearby passengers on the flight helping to hold the infants. Everyone felt sorry for her. People would have understood if she had drifted into self-pity, complaining how unfair life had been to her and blamed her husband for her plight. But Suzy says "I never allowed myself to wonder how my life would be if I only had one baby. I knew that wouldn't be productive. I had the fabulous four. I had to accept what was real."

Suzy says her humor helped her be resilient. Today her four children are college educated, starting their own lives, and she has a great job as a director of a state office that helps film makers. Looking back on the entire experience, she says "there were tough times, but I'd do it again because the good far outweighed the bad!"

Life's best survivors get better and better with age. Like cats, they manage to land on their feet when the bottom drops out of their lives.

Drawbacks of Unexpressed Emotions

Did you lose a job through no fault of your own? Been transferred or reassigned in a very insensitive way? Have you been through a divorce that now makes your life more difficult than you ever expected?

Have you dealt with your emotions about these life disrupting events? It is important to consciously uncover and acknowledge your feelings because *if you haven't resolved your angry feelings, you will not be able to study, not become involved with your new life direction, and you will be less effective in employment interviews.*

Strong unresolved feelings have more power over you than feelings you have expressed and "processed." People who don't allow themselves to feel and express strong emotions often experience flare-ups of anger, distrust, hostility, or despair.

The Benefits of Expressing Upsetting Emotions

If you find yourself sitting in class, and haven't heard anything the instructor said for ten minutes because you've been holding an internal emotional conversation with people who disrupted your life, you need to do something.

Psychologist James Pennebaker was asked to help a group of professional people who had been laid off and were unable to find work. He put them in a conference room and had them write about their deepest thoughts and feelings surrounding the layoff and how their lives had been affected. They wrote as fast as they could without regard for spelling or neatness. They did this for about twenty minutes a day five days in a row.

Three months later 23% of the group had full-time employment. Eight months later 53% had full-time employment, several more had satisfactory part-time employment, and one had started his own business. When interviewed, they all said they found the experience of writing about their feelings so helpful *they wished they had been made to do it much sooner!*

Mentally healthy people express angry feelings and grieve their losses as part of their transition to a new life. If you haven't dealt with upsetting losses, start writing about your feelings.

The Counseling Center Can Help

Most college students have periods of feeling lonely and depressed. If this happens to you, remember that such feelings are part of being human. School counselors can show you how to get through an unpleasant period while the natural emotional processes of self-healing are operating.

Emotional upsets are normal. You don't have to handle

them alone. It is not a sign of strength to mask your feelings with drugs or put on a front of happiness. Emotional strength develops from feeling whatever you feel and talking to friends when things aren't working well. Get some help from your friends, family, and other resources when things aren't so great.

Professionalism is Replacing Job Descriptions

People who thrive in constant change do not need detailed job descriptions. They have a strong attitude of professionalism that lets them find ways to be useful and successful in new and ambiguous situations.

Changes in the workplace now occur so rapidly it is rare for anyone to have an up-to-date job description. Some corporations have stopped giving people job descriptions. They have job categories for determining compensation levels, but they now rely on people who know how to make themselves useful, work well with others, and are constantly adapting and learning. Employers are searching for people with professionalism.

How to Increase Your Resiliency and Professionalism

Years of research shows that there is a strong similarity between a person with professionalism and a person who gains strength from life's difficult experiences. A person with the following qualities and personality traits is most likely to succeed and thrive in a rapidly changing, sometimes unfair world.

Create Good Synergy: Focus on Making Things Work Well

People with the most resiliency in times of change are those who need and expect difficult situations to eventually work out all right. They create a good "flow" in their part of the world. They get maximum results with minimum time and energy. The way they interact with people and situations has a synergistic effect. That is why they are good people to have around. They have a knack for knowing what to focus on and what to ignore, what to stick with and what to change.

Needing to have things work well makes a person comfortable with constant change. Having things work better requires giving up or changing old practices, assumptions, and beliefs. When better ways of doing things come along, people with professionalism adopt them easily.

This need for good synergy is the internal, organizing frame of reference for thriving in ambiguous, new, changing, situations. When faced with a disruptive situation a person avoids reacting like a victim by thinking "How can I interact with this so that things work out well for everyone?"

Child-Like Curiosity is a Survival Skill

To handle change or a disruptive situation well, you must read the new reality rapidly. You must quickly and accurately understand and comprehend what is happening.

Being open to read, assess, and respond to new developments is a reflex in people who adapt faster and better than others. It is a brain habit based on retaining a childlike curiosity throughout one's life.

Do you ask lots of questions? Wonder how things work? Wonder how and why other people do what they do?

This sort of curiosity gives a person a mind that quickly comprehends upsetting developments and changes that bewilder others. People who thrive in a changing world are accustomed to what is unusual, complicated, and mysterious. That is why, when hit with disruptive change and unexpected difficulties, they quickly absorb information about what is happening.

Playful Humor Makes a Big Difference

Threats and crises can trigger a person's inborn "fight or flight" response. A strong surge of adrenaline can increase the speed of your muscular reflexes and your muscle strength, but it impairs good problem solving. That is why laughing or joking during a crisis is very practical!

Why does humor help? Laughing reduces tension. Creative problem solving, accurate thinking, and good physical coordination are best in moderate emotional states. Alan Alda's irreverent humor as Hawkeye in the television series "M.A.S.H." was an excellent example. He was serious about being a surgeon but not about being a soldier. Hawkeye's sense of humor is typical of people who are best at dealing with emergencies and dicey situations.

The humor is not hostile or hurtful. It is directed toward the situation. The person toys with what is happening and pokes fun at it. Chances for surviving are increased by the attitude, "I am bigger than this situation. This is my toy. I am going to play with it."

Humorous playing is a way of asking "How does this look from a different point of view? What would happen if I turned it upside down? What if the reverse were true? What unusual things exist here?" By playing and toying with the situation, the person avoids being overwhelmed and at the same time is likely to come up with a way to survive.

How about you? Have you ever been poked in the ribs for muttering a humorous comment during a serious moment? If so, that is a good sign.

Be Adaptable and Flexible

Survivors of extreme adversity say that the most important quality in survival is to be flexible and adaptable. A person must be able to do something different than they ever did before, perhaps even the opposite.

What makes inner flexibility possible? Counterbalanced personality traits. They let you be both one way *and* the opposite, both pessimistic and optimistic, for example.

Can a person be both? Yes. Life's best survivors are comfortable with their paradoxical qualities even though the popular thinking is that people are either one way or the other, such as either pessimistic *or* optimistic.

Paradoxical or counter-balanced personality traits are something like having both extensor and flexor muscles in your arm. You can make your arms, hands, and fingers do what you want because you control the choice point between two sets of opposing muscles.

How flexible and paradoxical are you? Look at the two lists on the following page. Check off the traits you possess. Add traits not listed in the spaces at the bottom.

- [ ] calm
- [ ] trusting
- [ ] strong
- [ ] serious
- [ ] lazy
- [ ] stingy
- [ ] curious
- [ ] self-confident
- [ ] pessimistic
- [ ] unselfish
- [ ] _____
- [ ] _____

- [ ] emotional
- [ ] cautious
- [ ] gentle
- [ ] playful
- [ ] hard-working
- [ ] generous
- [ ] indifferent
- [ ] self-critical
- [ ] optimistic
- [ ] selfish
- [ ] _____
- [ ] _____

If you looked at the lists and quickly decided "All of the above, depending on the situation," that's wonderful. If you wrote down several more pairs of paradoxical or contradictory qualities you've noticed about yourself, that is an *excellent* sign.

It is important to understand that the lists are not meant to be a comprehensive listing of all possible pairs. The two lists are there to demonstrate an important point. Being paradoxical gives you flexibility and the more pairs of paradoxical traits you have, the more flexible you are at dealing with any situation that develops. If you identify with having many such contradictory traits you will have many more pairs than those listed.

Having opposing personality traits is like having a reverse gear in a car. It lets you back up when you need to. People without many counter-balanced or paradoxical pairs of traits are emotionally handicapped. They are rigid and inflexible because they were trained to be one-sided. They were taught to never be selfish, angry, negative, lazy, or self-appreciating.

One-sided people are difficult to live and work with. They have an energy draining effect on work teams. They are so concerned about acting as they think they should, they interfere with things working well.

It is also true that some people have so many contrary qualities they are flaky. They have an energy draining effect on work teams because they are emotionally scattered and disorganized. The professional person has found a way to exercise easy control over how and when to jump the tracks.

Both Creative and Traditional

Creativity is the ability to come up with a new way of doing things that works. The creativity essential for agility and thriving derives from the need to have things work well and having a paradoxical nature. The need to have things work well gives a person an inner frame of reference for choosing between doing something unusual or staying with what is working quite well. This is why people with highly developed professionalism are both creative and traditional in the way they work.

Practice Intuition and Empathy

The people who thrive in a variety of situations trust their intuition and have good empathy skills. They monitor their own internal emotional state and can read the emotional states of others as well.

Coping with new situations often depends on a sense that something is wrong. A tight stomach or an uneasy feeling may be the clue. These feelings can be set off by anything—a person's tone of voice, something not said, a group's quietness, anything at all that doesn't fit.

Women are usually better than men at using intuition because most women are raised practicing it. Men who practice intuition can develop the same ability, however, because it is based on subliminal perception—something that exists within every human.

People who handle others well are able to step out of their own feelings and views to empathize with the feelings and perceptions of others. As you will see if you view our web site file "Career Choice," people most likely to be successful in job interviews start by conducting interviews about the organization they would like to look for. A company won't hire you because you need money to pay your bills. They may hire you if you can present yourself as having skills they need.

Empathy does *not* mean you are a weak, easily hurt bleeding heart. Survivor empathy is the kind Abraham Lincoln used during his years as a defense attorney. He was very successful because he would begin his opening statements to the jury presenting a better case against his client than the opposing attorney was prepared to do.

Here is an example of how empathy led an electronics specialist to remain working for a corporation even though his job was eliminated through downsizing. One morning he was informed by his manager that his position was being eliminated. The specialist knew his work was critical for completing an important new product. He looked at the situation from the perspective of the managers and executives. He saw that they needed someone with his skills. He inquired about how the company would get essential work done without employees qualified to do it. He learned that consultants would be hired.

He wrote up his qualifications to be a consultant to the company and made an appointment with the project engineer. He explained how critical his skills were. The engineer agreed and arranged to hire him as a consultant. The man says he remained at his same work station and kept on doing the same work.

Empathy includes understanding people who live and think in disliked ways, including the manager who may have laid you off. The attitude of the empathy described here is "whether I like you or dislike you, I am going to understand you as well as you understand yourself—and maybe better."

Change Requires Learning

If you look in an introductory psychology textbook you will find that "Learning" will usually be defined as "A relatively permanent change in behavior that results from experience."

Do you see the point? Change and learning go together. You

can't have one without the other. Learning leads to change; change requires learning.

When faced with life or job changes that no parent or teacher prepared you for, you must manage your learning by asking questions and finding your own answers. To react to life as a school means to ask questions such as:

Why did they do that? What do they believe will be accomplished? What do I need to do differently now? How are certain important things going to get done?

Professional people and people who thrive learn valuable lessons from bad experiences. Here are the steps to follow:

1. Ask "What happened?"
2. Replay the incident as an observer.
3. Describe what happened. Put it into words.
4. Ask "What can I learn from this? What is the lesson here?"
5. Ask "Next time, what will I do differently?"
6. The next time a person says that to me, what will I say?
7. Imagine yourself handling the situation well the next time.
8. See and feel yourself getting the outcome you desire.
9. Rehearse the effective response.

When you follow these steps for self-managed learning, you will increase your self-confidence and look forward to the next incident with positive anticipation. In contrast, a person who dwells on a past experience with anger and distress anticipates the next incident with dread and does not expect a good outcome. This is why whatever you expect to happen, whether good or bad, usually determines the way things turn out.

Keep Learning in the School of Life

Abraham Maslow is quoted as saying that no one achieves full self-actualization until the age of sixty. He saw that people who constantly learn from experience get better and better decade after decade.

Your most valuable learning comes from the school of life. Throughout this book, whenever we addressed a difficult situation, our approach has been to show you that no matter what happens, you have the inborn ability to handle the difficulty in a way that makes you a stronger, more capable person.

Find a Way to Convert Misfortune into Good Fortune

You may have heard the word *serendipity*. Horace Walpole coined the term to describe a person having the *wisdom* to see that an *accident* or unfortunate development is actually a stroke of *good fortune*.

Your talent for serendipity comes from asking questions such as "Why is it good that this happened?" "What is the gift this brings me?" "What problem does this solve?"

Perhaps you have heard someone say that losing their job, getting cancer, or being divorced was one of the best things that ever happened to them. Can you look back at a rough situation and appreciate that it was also good for you?

We humans have the ability to find value in bad experiences and convert misfortune into good luck. The better you are at thriving and practicing professionalism, the more you will avoid reacting to disruptive change like a victim and can find the joy of serendipity in rough situations.

Action Review: HOW RESILIENT ARE YOU?*

Rate yourself from 1 to 5 on the following:
(1 = very little, 5 = very strong)

__ Adapt quickly to change. Good at bouncing back from difficulties.

__ Optimistic, see difficulties as temporary and feel determined to overcome them. Expect things to turn out well.

__ In a crisis I calm myself and focus on taking useful actions.

__ Play with new developments, find the humor, laugh at self, chuckle.

__ Curious, ask questions, want to know how things work, experiment.

__ Constantly learn from experience and from the experiences of others.

__ Very flexible. Feel comfortable with inner complexity (trusting and cautious, unselfish and selfish, optimistic and pessimistic, etc.)

__ Anticipate problems to avoid them and expect the unexpected.

__ Feel self-confident, enjoy healthy self-esteem, and have an attitude of professionalism about work.

__ Good listener. Good empathy skills. "Read" people well. Non-judgmental (even with difficult people). Can adapt to various personality styles.

__ Think up creative solutions to challenges, invent ways to solve problems. Trust intuition, hunches.

__ Able to recover emotionally from losses and setbacks. Can express feelings to others, let go of anger, overcome discouragement, ask for help.

__ Very durable, keep on going during tough times. Have a stabilizing effect on others during periods of ambiguity, uncertainty, and turmoil.

__ Have been made stronger and better by difficult experiences.

__ Convert misfortune into good fortune. What is the unexpected benefit?

======
__ Total

Scoring: 60-70—highly resilient!
50-60—better than most
40-50—slow, but adequate
30-40—you're struggling
30 or under—seek help!

© 1999, Al Siebert, PhD.

*This quiz is adapted from *The Survivor Personality* by Al Siebert, Ph.D.

⎍ An explanation of the items can be found by clicking on "Survivor Personality Quiz" at the Adult Student web site: http://www.adultstudent.com/

Support Group Activity

Describe from your own experience the difference between people who thrive well in difficult situations and people who can turn an ordinary day into a horrible experience.

Describe the difference between people who bring an attitude of professionalism to their work and people who are qualified, but have an unprofessional attitude.

Talk with each other about your reaction to learning it is desirable to have paradoxical personality traits. Were you raised to be one way but not the opposite? Trained to be a "good" child?

Tell each other about one of the worst experiences of your life and what you learned or gained from it. Take your time. Let each person finish before anyone else starts their story.

Resources and Selected Reading

Chapter 1

Sher, Barbara, and Gottlieb, Annie. *Teamworks!* New York: Warner Books, 1991. Contains valuable guidelines for forming and running a support group.

Chapter 2

Bob DePrato quote from *Your Hidden Credentials*, by Peter Smith. Washington, DC: Acropolis Books, 1986, p. 67. An encouraging book for adult students.

Eva Corazon Fernando-Lumba quote from *The Oregonian*, May 30, 1991.

Chapter 3

Ekstrom, Ruth B.; Harris, Abigail M., and Lockheed, Marlaine E. *How to Get College Credit for What You Have Learned as a Homemaker and Volunteer.* Princeton, NJ: Educational Testing Service.

Ronald E. Lemay story in *The Christian Science Monitor*, April 24, 1987. Center section.

Foundation Center. *Grants for Minorities.* New York: Foundation Center, 1990.

To read more about Carol Sasaki, see "From Welfare to Work Force" by Chris Phillips in *Family Circle*, Oct. 11, 1988.

Article about Gerald Winterlin, "We're Not Bums," appeared in *Parade Magazine*, May 13, 1991, p. 8.

U. S. Department of Education. *The Student Guide,* 1991.

Hechinger, Grace. "Will Your Company Pay for Your Classes?" *Glamour Magazine*, Feb. 1987.

A good book on sources of money for adult students is *Paying for Your Education: A Guide for Adult Learners*. Copies may be purchased from College Board Publication Orders, P.O. Box 2815, Princeton, NJ 08541.

Chapter 4

Edna Mae Pitman quote from *The Oregonian*, Jan. 1989.

Chapter 5

Lakein, Alan. *How to Get Control of Your Time and Your Life*. New York: New American Library, 1973. A classic in the field. Lakein shows how to establish priorities for yourself, choose activities that are of highest value to you, and minimize the amount of time you put into low payoff activities. If your school has an audiovisual library, it may have a copy of the film based on this book. You can arrange to preview the film. Take a few friends.

Adelizzi, Jane Utley, and Goss, Diane B. (Eds.) *A Closer Look: Perspectives and Reflections on College Students with Learning Disabilities*. Milton, MA: Curry College Press, 1995. Information about this book and the Curry College PAL program for college students with learning disabilities is available on-line at: http://www.curry.edu:8080/pal/files/new.html

Chapter 6

McKeachie, Wilbert J.; Pollie, Donald, and Speisman, Joseph. "Relieving Anxiety in Classroom Examination." *Journal of Abnormal and Social Psychology*. Vol. 50, No. 1, Jan. 1955, pp. 93-98.

Chapter 7

Strunk, William, Jr., and White, E. B. *The Elements of Style*. New York: Macmillan, 1972. This book can be valuable to anyone wanting to improve the quality and clarity of written communications. It shows how to use good grammar, punctuate correctly, and write clearly.

Chapter 8

Chapman, Elwood N. *Your Attitude Is Showing.* Chicago: Science Research Associates, Inc., an IBM company, 1987.

Keirsey, David, and Bates, Marilyn. *Please Understand Me.* Del Mar: Prometheus Nemesis Book Co., 1984.

Brown, Virginia, and DeCoster, David. "The Myers-Briggs Type Indicator as a Developmental Measure: Implications for Student Learners in Higher Education." *Journal of College Student Development*, July 1991.

Hays, Pamela and Ellis R. *Communication Activities for Personal Life Strategies.* Dubuque, Iowa: Kendall/Hunt Publishing Company, 1989.

Murray, Bridget. "Professor's Most Grating Habits." *Monitor on Psychology,* American Psychological Association, Vol. 31, No.1, Jan. 2000, pp. 56-57.

Chapter 9

Mendelsohn, Pam. *Happier by Degrees.* New York: Dutton, 1980. Practical advice for women in college who have families. Covers how student mothers become better mothers; how husbands and children react and think; being a single parent; and advice from husbands of college students to other husbands.

"Taking Charge" and other articles on "How to Reinvent Your Life," *Modern Maturity*, Jan/Feb, 2000, pp 26-45.

Chapter 10

Eurich, Neil. *Corporate Classrooms: The Learning Business.* Princeton, NJ: Princeton University Press, 1985.

Conroy, Mary. "Co-operative Education: Learn-and-Earn College Programs." *Better Homes & Gardens,* May 1987.

Eliason, Carol. "Co-op Can Make a Difference to Fledgling Entrepreneurs." *Workplace Education*, Sept.-Oct. 1984.

Chapter 11

Barringer, F., "Changing Picture of Metropolitan America," *The New York Times*, Aug. 1, 1992.

Brookfield, Stephen, *The Skillful Teacher,* Jossey-Bass Inc., 1990.

"Diversity in the U.S. College Population," *Chronicle of Higher Education*, Mar.18, 1992.

Naisbitt, John, *Megatrends Asia,* Simon and Schuster. New York, 1996.

Roueche, J. and Roueche, S. *Between a Rock and a Hard Place*, The American Association of Community Colleges, Washington, D.C., 1993.

Chapter 12

Colgrove, Melba, Ph.D., Bloomfield, Harold, M.D., and McWilliams. Peter. *How to Survive the Loss of Love,* Los Angeles: Prelude Press, 1976, 1991.

Flach, Frederic. *Resilience: Discovering A New Strength at Times of Stress.* New York: Fawcett Columbine, 1988.

Siebert, Al. *The Survivor Personality*, Berkeley/Perigee, New York, 1996.

Chapter 13

This chapter is adapted from *The Survivor Personality*, by Al Siebert. Berkeley/Perigee, New York, 1996, and was first published on Siebert's THRIVE*net* internet site, http://www.thrivenet.com/.

Kipplinger Washington Letter, December 22, 1999, "Your education won't stop when you leave high school or college. You'll be a life-long learner—classes at night, at work, or on the Net . . . You will rely more on your own wits and resources for success than previous generations. Employer and government safety nets will shrink."

Aitken, Sandi, and Morgan, John, "How Motorola Promotes Good Health," in *The Journal For Quality and Participation*, Jan/Feb, 1999, pp. 54-57.

Day, Laura. *Practical Intuition for Success.* New York: HarperCollins, 1997.

Pulley, Mary Lynn, and Deal, Terrance E. *Losing Your Job—Reclaiming Your Soul: Stories of Resilience, Renewal, and Hope.* Jossey-Bass, 1997.

Rubin, Bonnie Miller. "Secrets of Resilient Women," *Good House-keeping*, January, 2000, pp. 108-111.

Ury, William. *Getting Past No*. New York: Bantam Books, 1991. A practical book on how to develop empathy for opponents.

Read more about Diana Spatz, Paul Weiand, Jackie Leno Grant, and Suzy Kellett in the "Past Stories of the Month" file at the THRIVE*net* website: http://www.thrivenet.com/

Career Search Books:

Bridges, William. *Transitions: Making Sense of Life's Changes.*

Gross, Pam and Peter Paskill. *Want a New, Better, Fantastic Job?*

Irish, Richard. *Go Hire Yourself an Employer.*

Knoke, William. *Bold new World: The Essential Road Map to the Twenty-First Century.*

Mitchell, Charlie and Lauren Collins. *Job Hunting.*

Peterson's Guides On-Line has up-to-date job market and job search information. Their current book list includes: *Top 2500 Employers, Hidden Job Market 2000, Job Seeker's Almanac,* and *The Ultimate Job Search Survival Guide.* http://www.petersons.com/

Porcino, Jane. *Growing Older, Getting Better: A Handbook for Women in the Second Half of Life.*

Russell Nave, Jean and Louise M. Nelson. *Mid-Career Crisis.*

Sheckley, Lamdin, & Keeton. *Employability in a High Performance Economy.*

Witt, Melanie Astaire. *Job Strategies for People With Disabilities.* Peterson's Guides.

Online Resources

The following internet sites provide a range of useful information for college students. Much of what is listed are not-for-profit or educational organizations. We included some commercial listings with useful and accessible information. Check the sites periodically for new information. Check our Adult Student site for additional links and updates:

⏦ http://www.adultstudent.com/

General College Resources:
Sites such as magazines, newspapers and television stations often have areas and resources for college students. Try Newsweek.com, Time.com, and USAToday.com as starters.

US Department of Education:
http://www.ed.gov/
College Board Online:
http://www.collegeboard.org/
Education Index:
http://www.educationindex.com/lifestage.html

Adult Student Resources:
Back2College:
http://www.back2college.com/
Office of Adult Learning Services (College Board Online):
http://www.collegeboard.org/offals/html/indx001.html
Texas A&M Adult and Grad Student Services:
http://stulife.tamu.edu/agss/
Nontraditional students defined:
http://www.ed.gov/databases/ERIC_Digests/ed347483.html

Financial Aid Resources:
US Dept of Education, financial info:
http://www.ed.gov/prog_info/SFA/StudentGuide/
fastWEB (a FREE scholarship matching service):
http://www.fastweb.com/

Financial Aid Resources:
http://www.finaid.org/
The Consumer Information Center:
http://www.pueblo.gsa.gov/education.htm
Educaid:
http://www.educaid.com/
Strategies for the Non-Traditional Student:
http://www.freschinfo.com/strategy%2Dnontrad.phtml
Sallie Mae loan servicer information page:
http://www.salliemae.com/aud/adult.html
Chinook College Funding Service:
http://www.chinook.com/index.html
Cash for College:
http://www.nasfaa.org/public/cashfc.html
College is Possible (American Council on Education):
http://www.collegeispossible.org/paying/paying.htm

Disabled Student Resources:
Succeeding in College with ADD at 30, 40, 50—Yes!:
http://www.addvance.com/article4.html
Program for Advancement of Learning from Curry College:
http://www.curry.edu:8080/pal/pal.html
National Center for Learning Disabilities College Resources:
http://ncld.org/resources/resources3.html
National Council on Disability "The Impact of Exemplary Technology-Support Programs on Students With Disabilities":
http://www.ncd.gov/publications/techsupport.html

Distance Learning Resources:
PBS Adult Learning Service:
http://www.pbs.org/als/
Distance Education Resources:
http://www.uwex.edu/disted/resources.html
Distance Education Frequently Asked Question Archive:
http://www.faqs.org/faqs/education/distance-ed-faq/

Channel3000 Distance Education info:
　　http://www.channel3000.com/education/distance_ed/
US Universities with online presences, by state:
　　http://www.utexas.edu/world/univ/state/#toc
Sample colleges with online presence:
Marylhurst University:
　　http://www.marylhurst.edu/
SW Missouri State University:
　　http://smsuonline.smsu.edu/
Portland Community College:
　　http://www.distance.pcc.edu/

Portfolio:
Portfolio Library:
　　http://www.amby.com/kimeldorf/portfolio/

Career Search / Basic Job Resources:
America's Job Bank:
　　http://www.ajb.dni.us/
Career Mosaic:
　　http://www.careermosaic.com/
Career Web:
　　http://www.cweb.com/
Career Mosaic:
　　http://www.careermosaic.com/
Gopher Jewels:
　　http://galaxy.einet.net/GJ/employment.html
Jobtrack:
　　http://www.jobtrak.com/
Jobweb:
　　http://www.jobweb.com/
Online Career Center:
　　http://www.occ.com/occ/
National Commission for Co-Operative Education:
　　http://www.co-op.edu/
The Riley Guide: Employment Opportunities and Job Resources on the Internet:

http://www.dbm.com/jobguide/
Amby's Work Site:
http://www.amby.com/worksite/

Reference Resources:
Library of Congress Online:
http://lcweb.loc.gov/
Microsoft Encarta Encyclopedia:
http://encarta.msn.com/
US. Census Bureau:
http://www.census.gov/
List of Public Libraries with Web Servers:
http://sjcpl.lib.in.us/homepage/PublicLibraries/
PubLibSrvsGpherWWW.html
One state's Online Library:
DelAWARE library reference page:
http://www.lib.de.us/delaweb/reference.shtml
Internet Public Library:
http://www.ipl.org/
About.com Reference library list:
http://librarians.about.com/business/librarians/
msubref.htm
National Archives and Records Administration:
http://www.nara.gov/
Learning Link:
http://learninglink.net/Reference/

Miscellaneous:
Self-Help Counseling Center, University of Buffalo:
http://ub-counseling.buffalo.edu/selfhelp.html
Study Skills Self Help:
http://www.ucc.vt.edu/stdysk/stdyhlp.html
Study tips from UC Berkley:
http://128.32.89.153/CalRENHP.html
ERIC Online (Educational Resources Information Center):
http://www.accesseric.org/

Sample Searchng Keywords:

Use the following keywords at your favorite internet searching site:

> adult college student, adult learner, re-entry student, returning student, distance learning, continuing education, college student, student orientation, campus counseling center, career change, study, student success, college funding, financial aid, grants, scholarships.

Some popular sites are: *AltaVista.com, Ask.com, Dogpile.com, Excite.com, Google.com, Lycos.com, Northernlight.com, Search.com, Snap.com, StartingPoint.com, Yahoo.com.*

Searching Tips:

✦ **Use the "back" button on your browser**, or alternately, the "History" or "Go" menus. The "back" button will take you to the last page you visited. This will come in handy if you performed a search on a search engine and want to get back to the list of returned sites with out having to type in the search again.

✦ **Use a multi-search engine to start:** *www.dogpile.com, www.about.com, www.go2net.com* or similar are good ones to try. They will search a number of other search engines for their top matches. You may get duplicate listings, but you'll get a feel for which engine is providing you with the best matches for your query. If you want more listings from any one search engine, you can then visit the ones that have the most relevant data.

✦ **Browse the search engine's directory:** Most search engines not only allow you to search the web for your term, but have already categorized listings of sites related to your question. Check the "Education" category on *Yahoo.com*, for example.

✦ **Explore the sites you visit.** If you find a single page article that has useful information on it, take the time to explore what else the site offers. Hit their Home Page link, or "backstep" as described below in "404 FileNot Found."

- ✦ **Use the site's built-in search engine.** Many sites incorporate their own on-site search engine. These are very useful for finding the specific information you might be after. Use your browser's "find" command to search for a term on the page you're browsing. This is useful on a page with a lot of content.

- ✦ **Server busy error:** This usually indicates that the server (a computer "hosting" the file or site) you're wanting is either temporarily not functioning, overloaded, or the pathway to the server is obstructed somehow. Try to access the site at a later time.

- ✦ **Unable to locate a server:** This usually means that the server is no longer in service, that you made a typing error, or the address wasn't quite right. Sometimes, though, the big routing servers go down and computers from a certain region may not be able to "find" the address you want to go to. Try again later or check whether the domain name (server name) is valid. Do this by visiting *http://www.whois.net/* for a "who is" searching gateway. You can type in the domain name and it will return a screen that tells you if and to whom the domain name has been registered.

- ✦ **"404 File not found" error** when trying to access a site means that the server is working, but that the specific file is no longer available. Sometimes the owner of the file has changed services or reconstructed the site. If the owner has moved, you will have to search the title of the file on a search engine. If the site has been reorganized, you may be able to find the file you want by backstepping the cursor in the address line deleting the characters back to a "/" mark and hitting "enter" again. Keep doing this until you get to a spot where a real page is displayed and look for the file you want.

- ✦ **A good computer book for beginners** is *Teach Yourself Computers and the Internet Visually, 2nd Edition,* IDG Books Worldwide, Inc., Foster City, CA: 1998.

Internet Glossary

Attachment: a file sent "attached" to an e-mail message. May be a picture, text file, audio, video, or executable program. Multiple files may be "stuffed" or "zipped" in order to save space and protect the data from corruption.

Browser: software program used to view Web pages, also may include e-mail and ftp functionality.

Chat: real-time discussions at your computer using your keyboard, either at a web site or using stand-alone software.

Directory: a searchable internet site which categorizes web sites and lists links, often with a review. *About.com* is an example of a directory. Often directories will have search engine abilities as well.

Domain: in an internet address, the part of the naming convention that consists of a sequence of characters separated by dots. The fivemost common types of domains are: ".com" for company or commercial entity, ".org" for non-profit organization, ".gov" for government agency, ".net" for a network, and ".edu" for educational institution. An internet site's full domain name would be "sitename.com" or "sitename.org" for example. Two sites with such similar names are registered as two separate sites and may or may not be operated by the same company.

E-mail: electronic mail sent over the internet or online service through a stand alone software program or integrated browser.

FTP: File Transfer Protocol. This is the technical term for "uploading" and "downloading" files from a server. These files can not usually be viewed by the browser software. Current browsers integrate FTP into their software, or you may use a stand alone program.

HTML (HyperText Markup Language): the predominent programming language used to write web pages.

Internet: global network of computers which allows people to share information via phone and digital data lines.

Link (hyperlink): the text or picture you click on to jump from one page or site to another.

Newsgroups: (also known as USENET) the internet's equivalent to the community bulletin board. *Deja.com* has a Web interface for searching and reading posts to newsgroups. Choose a category then select discussions.

Search Engine: a site on the Web which lets you search the internet using keywords or phrases.

Server: a computer with full-time access to the internet which is used to store files and web sites and "serve" them up as needed when accessed via a url.

Subdomain: first part of the internet naming construction which often describes the function of a site, or is used for organization. Common subdomains are: "www" for World Wide Web; "ftp" for file transfer protocol, "mail" for a mail server; etc. For example, www.adultstudent.com is a web site, while ftp.adultstudent.com would be an area for housing files available for download. Larger sites often will divide activities into subdomains, such as "search.aol.com" "mailaol.aol.com" or "shop.aol.com."

URL or Web Address: the uniform resource locator, or web address is the location of a specific web site. Most often beginning with "http://www." If you see a television commercial saying to visit "hotjobs.com", you must type the complete url: "http://www.hotjobs.com."

Virus: a program that can attack a personal computer in a variety of usually destructive ways. Viruses are spread by opening infected disks or files. Purchase anti-virus software and run it regularly. Also, do not open e-mail messages from someone you don't recognize.

Web page: one file as viewed through a browser window.

Web site: a collection of pages (or files) from one entity that are linked together.

World Wide Web (www, Web): multi-media interlinked function of the internet. Text, pictures, sound and video can be transmitted via the World Wide Web.

Index

active learning 35–36, 39
active recall 50
adaptable 141–143
anxiety 65–66
attitudes 42, 119–122
audit 13
auditory learning style 89–91

balancing work demands 115–117
basic income jobs 115

career search 156–157
catalog 21
changing world 136
child care services 14
classes at reduced cost 13, 27
college catalog 21
College Level Entrance Examination
    Program (CLEP) 25
common fears 9–19
communicate 102–103, 137–138
comprehension 52–56
computer courses 22
computer resources
    financial aid 28
    library searches 77
concentration span 56–57
cooperative work experience (CWE)
    112–113
counseling center 138–139
courseload 23, 111–112
creative 143
credit course 22
cultural
    difficulties 122–123
    diversity 118–125
curiosity 140

degrees 23
demographics 119–122
differences 95–96
direct loans 29–30
disabled students 50–51, 155
distance learning 22, 155
dropping class 26–27
dyslexia 11

empathy 143–144
employer aid 16–17, 30, 110–117
ethnic diversity 118–125
expectations 122–124
extroversion 92–95

family 116
    and friends 100–109
    expectations 123
    members 14, 15
fears 9–19
feedback to instructors 96
financial aid 13–14, 26–30, 154–155
financial aid form (FAF) 28
flexible 136–137, 141–143
follow directions 82–83
full-time student 23

gaining support 100–109
GI benefits 29
goals 39–40
    life 39–40
    study 44
"good child" handicap 131–132
grade point average (GPA)
    how to calculate 83
grades 12–13
grants 28–30

home study 14
humor 140

incomplete 97
instructors 64, 76, 96–99
    influencing 96–99
    reward 98
internet 78
internet glossary 160
internship 114
introversion 92–95
intuition 94, 143–144

journals 77–79

keeping on schedule 44–47

learning
    from experience 144–146
    principles 49–50, 58–59
    trouble 50–51
    disabilities 11, 50
learning styles 87–99, 98
    auditory 89–91
    external 88–89
    internal 88–89
    tactile 89–91, 91
    visual 89–91
lecture notes 37–38
left-brain 93–94
library 77–79
long essay questions 70–71

magazines 77–79
managing change 135–148
mandatory breaks 57–60
matching questions 69
"melting pot" 119–122
mix study subjects 58
multiple-choice question 68–69

noisy distractions 48
non-credit course 22
non-judgmental thinking 93–95, 120
note-taking 37–38
    mapping 38
    outline format 38
    summary method 38

old exams 63
online courses 22
organize 36–37

paradoxes 141–146
part-time student 14–15, 23
passive recognition 50
periodicals 77–78
plagiarism 81–82
positive action plan 96–98, 108,
    130–133
practice tests 62, 64–66
    advantages 66–67
practicum training experience 114–5
prerequisite course 21
pressure 126–134
principles of learning 49–50, 58–59
prior learning assessment (PLA) 24
professionalism 139

questions 9–19, 51–56, 76–79
    during an exam 73

racial diversity 118–125
recall tests 70–71
recognition tests 68–69
record study time 57
references 157
resiliency 136–144
revitalizing activities 132–133
reward instructors 96
right-brain 93–94

schedule of classes 21
scheduling
    steps 43–46
    work and school 111–112
self-chosen goals 39–40
self-esteem 131
self-managed learning 145–146
self-stopper 45, 57
serendipity 146
short answer test 71
social expectations 123–124
spouse/partner 15, 103–106
"stir fry" 124
stress 126–134
    misunderstanding about 127–128
    pressures 15
    resistant personalities 128–129
student
    employment 30
    help 113
student manual
    catalog 21
    workbooks 63–64
study
    area 48
    breaks 57–60
    goals 44
    habits 58
    techniques 43–60, 51–56
Study Buddies. *See* support groups
"study buddies"
    formation 15
studying at home 48–49
success
    in class 35
    on tests 62
successful students 34–41
support for family 106–109

support from family 101–105
support group
    creating 17–19
    hints for success 18–19
support group activity
       19, 33, 40, 60, 74, 84, 99,
       109, 117, 125, 134, 148
surprises 141–146
synergy 139–140
synthesis tests 71–72

tactile learning style 89–91
taking tests 11, 61–74
television 49
temperament 91–95
    extrovert 92
    feeling 93–94
    introvert 92
    intuition 94
    judging 94–95
    perceiving 94–95
    sensing 94
    thinking 93–94
test types 67
test-taking 61–74
    anxiety 65–66
    guidelines 67
tests
    open-book 71
    practice 62
    recall 70–71
    recognition 68
    synthesis 71–72
    take-home 71–72
textbooks 25–26
    reading 52–56
3 x 5 cards 54
time management 15, 43–60
"to do" lists 47
tour
    college 32
    neighborhood 31
transfer course 22
true-false questions 69

victim of instructors 95–96
visual learning style 89–91

web reference
    basic income job 115
    career choice 41

classroom listening 37
concentration 57
concerns and suggestions 16
financial aid 30
introduction 4
learning disabilities 11
note-taking samples 38
quiz explanation 147
support services 31
"Your Accomplishments Portfolio" 7
web-based courses 22
welfare success story 27
work study 113
working 110–117
worries 9–19
writing papers 75–84

Acknowledgements

This book is the result of the contributions of many people. We wish to express our special thanks to:

Timothy L. Walter for his many contributions to the early development of material in this book.

The instructors and counselors at Portland Community College for their encouragement, feedback, information, and suggestions.

Marcia House for her excellent professional secretarial skills.

Maris Bishoprick for keeping us current on developments in the library.

Clarice Anderson for financial aid information.

The students and instructors who critiqued the first, second and third editions and provided us with valuable feedback.

Teresa Rosen for her artistic skills and creativity.

George Vaterneck for many years of supportive mentoring.

Wilbert J. McKeachie and the University of Michigan psychology department faculty for creating a climate of professionalism in teaching.

John Gardner, Stuart Hunter, and the other Freshman Year Experience staff at the University of South Carolina for their dedication to first year students and their excellent stewardship.

Our families for their constant support and appreciation.

About the Authors

Al Siebert received his M.A. and Ph.D. in psychology at the University of Michigan. He has taught adult education classes for over 30 years. He is author of several "Student Success" books, host of the THRIVEnet web site, and author of *The Survivor Personality*.

Bernadine Gilpin started college at age thirty-five, with five children at home. She has a B.S. in education and an M.S. in counseling. For twenty years she served as instructor, administrator and counselor for adult students. She created and taught a college survival class over interactive TV and has written several books for adult students. Recent retirement from the college setting allows more time for writing. She currently is working on a book showing the power of positive parenting.

Mary Karr started college when the youngest of her four children started high school. She earned a B.S. in psychology and speech communication and her M.S. in speech communication. She teaches a college success seminar for re-entry students and created and teaches two communication courses on the internet for Marylhurst University.

Feedback Request

Please let us know how you did! How was *The Adult Student's Guide to Survival and Success* helpful to you? How did having a success group work out?

Do you have any suggestions on how *The Adult Student's Guide* could be improved? Write to us in care of:

Practical Psychology Press
PO Box 535
Portland, OR 97207

asg4@adultstudent.com

http://www.thrivenet.com/press.html

Also Available

Book:

THE SURVIVOR PERSONALITY: Why Some People Are Stronger, Smarter, and More Skillful at Handling Life's Difficulties...and How You Can Be, Too, by Al Siebert, PhD. (Foreword by Bernie Siegel, MD)
Berkley/Perigee Books, 1996. ISBN: 0-399-52230-1 $12

Videotape:

RESILIENCE: The Key to Surviving and Thriving in Today's World, by Al Siebert, PhD.
Practical Psychology Press, 1999. Color, 43 min. $25

Please add $2.00 for postage & handling. Send check or money order to:

> **Practical Psychology Press**
> **PO Box 535**
> **Portland, OR 97207**
>
> **press@thrivenet.com**

Satisfaction guaranteed.

For other books and resources about survivor resiliency, visit our sister web site at:

> **http://www.thrivenet.com/**